"Home is more than a room or walls and a roof, and Marlee walks us through this wonderful place of wonder and belonging that we all seek and need. *Living Spaces* is a tour of the heart—one you will treasure and not forget."

—Barbara Johnson, founder of Spatula Ministries,
best-selling author, Women of Faith speaker

"I have always loved houses, always felt as if each one could tell a special story. So it's no surprise that *Living Spaces* completely captivated me. This lovely book thoughtfully celebrates the spirit of home, creativity, function, and style. It's an inspiration on many levels. Beautifully done, Marlee!"

—Melody Carlson, author of Christy finalist *Finding Alice*,
and *Angels in the Snow*, *Armando's Treasure*, *Dark Blue*,
and *Diary of a Teenage Girl* books

"With deep insight and keen attention to details, Marlee takes readers on a fragrant journey into the true creation of home.

"One afternoon, after a three hour drive, I stopped by Marlee's just to say a quick hello. She dropped everything, poured two glasses of juice, and sat down across from me in a well-loved chair. In between us was a small table with a single candle. She reached over and lit the candle. I laughed and asked why she was lighting the candle in the middle of the day.

"With a smile, Marlee said, 'Because you're in my home. That's something to celebrate.'

"I never forgot the way she made me feel that day. Marlee knew how to do something mysteriously beautiful. She knew how to turn the ordinary into the sacred. With that same warmth of candlelight glow, Marlee brings to this book all the beauty of the sacred along with a road map so that the rest of us can find our way out of the ordinary all the way *home*."

—Robin Jones Gunn, best-selling author of the
Sisterchicks™ novels and *Tea at Glenbrooke*

"How much we all need and crave *home*. Marlee has used her gift for words and her gift of creating home to produce a treasure of a book. I love *Living Spaces*, and I know others will too."

—Nancie Carmichael, author of *Selah* and
founder of Virtue Live Ministries

"As one who is passionate about making our home the place where our bodies are nurtured, our souls are fed, and our spirits are sheltered, I embrace the message of Marlee's book. After knowing her, working with her, and enjoying her hospitality, I can assure her readers that the woman and the message are one."

—Ingrid Trobisch Youngdale, author of *Keeper of the Springs*
and *The Confident Woman*

Living SPACES
Bringing Style and Spirit to Your Home

Marlee LeDai

ILLUSTRATED BY LEYAH JENSEN

Revell
Grand Rapids, Michigan

Text © 2004 by Marlee LeDai
Illustrations © 2004 by Leyah Jensen

Published by Fleming H. Revell
a division of Baker Publishing Group
P.O. Box 6287, Grand Rapids, MI 49516-6287
www.revellbooks.com

Printed in the United States of America

Library of Congress Cataloging-in-Publication Data
LeDai, Marlee, 1948–
    Living spaces : bringing style and spirit to your home / Marlee LeDai.
       p.   cm.
    Includes bibliographical references.
    ISBN 0-8007-5889-7 (pbk.)
    1. Home—Religious aspects—Christianity. 2. Christian life—Meditations.
  I. Title.
  BR115.H56L43 2004
  248.4—dc22   2004009236

Dedicated to my parents,
Virginia Cook Smith
and Marvin Smith,
who always knew how to
make a house a home.

Contents

PART 3   THE DREAM HOME IN YOU

PART 4   ODE TO EVERYDAY EXTERIORS

An Invitation

Imagine yourself as a living house. God comes in to rebuild that house. At first, perhaps, you can understand what He is doing. He is getting the drains right and stopping the leaks in the roof and so on; you knew that those jobs needed doing and so you are not surprised. But presently He starts knocking the house about in a way that hurts abominably and does not seem to make sense. What on earth is He up to? The explanation is that He is building quite a different house from the one you thought of—throwing out a new wing here, putting on an extra floor there, running up towers, making courtyards. You thought you were being made into a decent little cottage: but He is building a palace. He intends to come and live in it Himself.

C. S. Lewis, *Mere Christianity*

Last week I went house hunting. My best friend had some advice for me just before I was to meet the Realtor. She said, "Don't look for what you can afford, Marlee. Look for what you love."

Those words rang in my mind as I headed out. The Realtor told me right off the bat, "I have a house I want you to see. It's brand-new and has just come on the market."

"No," I replied. "I'm not looking for 'new.' I'm looking for charm and history." Forgetting my friend's advice, I added, "Anyway, it sounds like it's out of my price range, so let's not waste time."

We looked at 1940s bungalows, a Victorian farmhouse, and beach-type cottages for most of a morning. Then, turning a corner, the Realtor said, "Oh, look; that's the house I wanted you to see."

Toward the end of a long street, a three-story castlelike home was being completed at the edge of a hillside. Its tall roof and round turret towered above the other homes.

I gasped. "That can't be the one you mentioned—that's not just out of my price range. That's more like a half-million-dollar house."

"You're right," she said. "Let's just check it out."

As we turned into the drive, confirming that it was the right address at the right price, we decided to go in just for the heck of it. How could my Realtor know that for two years I'd been journaling about building what I call a "prayer turret" onto the one-story house I live in? The addition would be a tall circular shape with a lofty view of stars and mountains. I would use it every morning to read, meditate, and pray. I knew exactly what it would look like.

Now, as I walked through the upper floor of the turret-house with the Realtor, I had come home, and I knew it. Spontaneously, unexpectedly, I said, "This is it. This is the house I want."

My dream home had materialized beyond my imagination. *How could it be,* I wondered, *that although I was looking for a bungalow, God had a palace in mind?*

The end of this story has not been written, because evidently the mortgage lender doesn't yet use the same criteria as God.

When I mentioned this to my friend, she said, "Don't just pray, 'Lord, I've done what I could do; now it's up to you.' Say, 'Lord, show me the way through the open doors.'"

Well, I am my own open door.

I've not yet moved into the home of my dreams, but that's not the point. Home is not about finding the perfect place to raise children, start a business, or retire. Neither is it about being a homemaker or decorating or remodeling a house. In fact, sometimes the most gracious homes are those for which we have no resources to spend on design and décor. Interior design is just what it says—design that comes from within, not without. It starts with me, no matter how much money I have to spend. It starts at the open front door.

I've heard Realtors say house hunting is about recognizing that certain indescribable something that makes one place feel more like home than another place. Yet somehow I've always been able to make myself at home wherever I am. This book is not about finding the right home or being *at* home as much as it is about being *a* home. Home happens when you hang out with yourself. Somehow, ultimately, we all know that. At the end of every day, we will come home, sit down, and put up our feet. We snuggle under covers if not into someone's arms. Home implies shelter—from the elements, strangers, and our troubles.

I've walked across the thresholds of a good many houses of different sizes, shapes, and cultural descriptions, recognizing them as home, whether I was going to be there a day or a year. While growing up, I lived in four different houses. As a young adult, I lived in a college dorm tucked into California's foothills, chalets in Switzerland and Austria, a basement in downtown Jerusalem, a church in Denmark, and an English manor house. While raising children, I lived in a brick villa, more than one row house, a thatched-roof homestead, a ranch-style house, and a woodsy cottage in the Northwest. For good or bad, each of these structures became home simply because it was invested with human presence—my own and the kindred spirits of people I love.

Most Americans live in three-bedroom, two-bath houses made of brick or wood in suburban neighborhoods. Some people live in cardboard boxes. Many live in concrete high-rise apartment buildings. A few live on rambling farms or ranches. More and more seem to be moving into gated communities where McMansions make Europe's palaces look pathetic.

Decorating firms, home accessory boutiques, furniture corporations, interior designers, and architects are having a heyday producing an array of products to meet the nesting instincts of home owners. We are a culture gone wild over the idea of transforming spaces. This can be good, yet there is something more to making a house a home.

This book is about that something more. It's not about *where* you live or *what kind* of home you live in. It's about *how* you live. Whether you paint it up or decorate it with sumptuous furnishings, home remains the place where you flesh out who you are and how you define the term "family circle."

Most of us think of home as the place with a welcome sign hanging out front, but home has so many more emotional overtones. It can be a four-letter word for some folks, a source of sad or bad memories. For others it brings the pain of wishing they could be there again, just once more. Since there is "no place like home," home will be different for every individual. Perhaps you're experiencing the loss of a home, coping with a broken home, selling your home, or just missing home. Homesickness comes in many guises. As bittersweet yearning, it implies the tangling together of loss and love. Its regret is tinged with nuances of hope.

Home may be where you stay in the bliss of domestic viability or what you take with you when you leave a particular address, perhaps escaping domestic bluster. What does the phrase "home sweet home" mean anyway? Is it just sentiment or something deeper? And when you do put down roots into the soil of a chosen location, what makes your house a home?

Explore these things with me and you'll find that home is a metaphor for your life—and mine. It is about recognizing that your house is beautiful just as it is, or as you want it to be, because you and God have taken up residence there.

These chapters contain more than information, reflection, explanation, and anecdote. They are crafted with you in mind: to make you remember, feel, and anticipate, to help you become motivated and energized. I hope the words set you to work on new dreams, enabling you to get closer to what you want from your home, in your home, and of your home.

Are you a down-home kind of person? We're not pretentious here. Take off your shoes, put up your feet, settle into a snug chair, and turn the page. Within these covers is a refuge. We're going to offer homage to the homes of our past, our present, and the future. Whether you are homeless, homebound, homespun, homely, or anything else, come with me. We're going to wonder about what Jesus had in mind when he said at the supper table, the very epicenter of home, "Anyone who loves me will keep my word; and my Father will extend love, and we will come and make our home with her."[1]

Jesus' invitation isn't about going to a heavenly home to be forever with the Lord. It's about God with us right here, right now. For though twilight falls, the porch light is on.

PART I

The Mystique
OF A HOUSE

ONE

The Threshold
OF EXPERIENCE

[Our house] had a heart, and a soul, and eyes to see us with; and approvals, and solicitudes, and deep sympathies; it was of us, and we were in its confidence, and lived in its grace and in the peace of its benediction.

Mark Twain

When my children were small, our family visited friends on a trip along the California coast. Eva, a mother of three, was recovering from chemotherapy and radiation treatments. Although she was unable to eat, she insisted on preparing brunch for us. The meal was wholesome and simple but lovingly served. Eva had been unable to garden that summer. Nevertheless, there were pansies on the table, plucked from the corners of her yard, and a fresh lemon off a backyard tree, sliced for our water glasses. Relaxing on patio furniture, we talked and laughed, sharing an hour of sunshine, wondering if we would meet again on this earth.

When the children and I got into our Ford Pinto to leave, my two-year-old climbed into the backseat and announced emphatically, "I like those people. They have a nice warm!"

My toddler defined that day the threshold where wood, brick, and mortar are transformed into sacred space. A threshold is both a point of entry and a level above which something is true and below which it is not. A "nice warm" sensed upon entering someone's home is not a matter of elaborate décor, parklike grounds, or gourmet cooking. It doesn't take loads of time, energy, or money. Our friend Eva didn't have those things. A "nice warm" starts with who you are, not with what you have. Engendered where your instinct for nesting meets your affection for other people, a "nice warm" is the threshold above which a house becomes a home.

If you wish to tap the enigma of what it means to emote a "nice warm," start by finding the sacred play in every day—right where you are with what you have in your hands. After all, a child's play is actually a child's work, isn't it? As a product of the 1950s and '60s, when domesticity reigned in my home, my personal amusement usually involved playing house wherever I found a bit of space and solitude. On a tree stump in the sun, I baked mud pies filled with grass and mud, sprinkled with pebbles. The best mud could be made by pouring a bucketful of water into the soil behind the garage and beside the alley. I let it soak and turned my attention to the hollyhocks growing around the garbage cans. My mother had taught me to make "ladies" of the blossoms—a large blossom for the skirt, a small one for the bodice, and a tiny one for the bonnet, all attached to the stem. These pink dolls decorated my tea table, a cardboard box where I later served mud concoctions to a three-year-old in briefs and cowboy boots. Soon my little brother was off again on his stick horse.

The spinster directly across from our home had a small white playhouse in her side yard. Immaculate and charming, it was the furthest thing from my mud dining room. Once she invited me, accompanied by my mother, inside. The playhouse was furnished with a child-sized table and chair set. On a doily lay dainty cups and saucers and a proper little teapot. It made me shiver with envy, although I had never seen anyone actually playing there. I never did hear the giggles of little girls spill out the windows. Perhaps the tiny cottage was just one woman's way to fulfill a childhood fantasy and create a "nice warm" in her own imagination.

As much as I wished for a fully outfitted playhouse in my backyard, I was of pioneer background, resourceful and inventive. I made do. In a corner of our screened back porch, behind Grandma Daisy's daybed, I walled in my own version, using chairs pulled from the kitchen. A shoe box lined with towels became my baby's crib. There were plenty of infant clothes left from my sister and me; so what if they were too big for my Betsy? An orange crate became a kitchen counter. I begged a few battered wooden spoons and other utensils from my mother. But once, looking for decorating inspiration in the Sears and Roebuck catalog, I came across an adorable dollhouse. Finger-sized beds and bathtubs—and people, a whole family of them! It was then I first experienced what yearning was—not daring to believe anything so wonderful could ever be mine.

But experts say it's never too late to have a happy childhood. I may never have the things I want from the Crate and Barrel catalog. Yet I cross the threshold for a "nice warm" by exploring the possibilities of making a home in the house I have. My house is red with white trim, a dark green door, and green window boxes. This year, with help from friends, I am going to make some changes: add scalloped shingles under the eaves, paint the exterior a cream color with white trim, and pull out all the stops for a bright red door.

My home is just a cottage, but it's located on an acre among ponderosa pines replete with singing birds. Blue and yellow wildflowers make their appearance in the spring. I often stop to appreciate the fact that although my house is not impressive, my eyes can roam an undomesticated landscape. Lots of critters play in the tall grass. From the office window at the back side of my home, I can see one of the smaller mountains in the Cascade range, Black Crater, snowcapped three seasons of the year. I keep on my desk the lava stones I picked up on a hike to its summit. They remind me that a view from the top—symbolizing the summits of my life—is worth the exhausting effort.

Occasionally my Pollyanna optimism about my humble residence gets deflated. I sometimes envy my close friend Abby, another single mom who lives nearby in a custom chateau with a view of the magnificent Three Sisters mountains. I know she too understands that a home is not about external realities but about the quality of perception and devotion. An attitude of passionate engagement combined with what is possible goes a long way. As much as I love dreaming over household wares from Pottery Barn and Restoration Hardware, I'm fully aware that a "nice warm" does not come out of a catalog or with a mountain view. It is helped along by mud-pie mentality, the kind of thinking that can create chocolaty confections from raw material at the end of the garden.

Corporate psychology tells us that businesses encouraging playfulness in the workplace are more productive and bottom-line effective. The principle can be applied elsewhere, not least of all in our daily routine of maintaining a home. The work goes easier with a dose of reverent play. Why not give free rein to this holy occupation? Amuse and entertain yourself within the walls of your home using what you already have to serve your family and guests.

"Bless what you do and what you have," I tell myself. See even the scarred, chipped, and weathered things as sacred—sacred because they bear to your family the significance of repetitive use in making a house a home. What could be more ordinary or profane, for example, than the family bathroom? The one in my house needs restoration badly. I finally noticed this when the last of my children left home. No longer distracted by the comings and goings of people constantly using this room, it became obvious that something was wrong. Using a large can of joint compound, I repaired the drywall where the commode tank sprayed water with each flush. After it dried I painted the buffeted walls a buttery yellow and the ceiling a bright white, then decorated the room with a dragonfly motif. Nothing short of winning a small lottery will allow me to fix the dilapidated sink and bathtub/shower used through fifteen years of hectic bedtime and morning rituals. I dream of brand-new Kohler faucets with elegant retro designs; it takes little to envision a sparkling white tile floor to replace the bruised and beaten linoleum.

Then I remember that old-fashioned "nice warm" doesn't cost a dime. I think back to the laughter in this tub when little pink bodies floated in iridescent foamy bliss. Who could forget the toilet overflowing during slumber parties to the hilarious shrieks of oodles of kids? Year after year the room was packed with giddy teenage girls doing one another's makeup and hair for proms. As I scrub aging bathroom fixtures with Ajax and all the playful attitude I can muster, I amuse myself by thinking of the family legacy that makes the profane profound.

Making a house a home is limited only by boundaries of re-sourcefulness and imagination, the soul of a structure. Creating a "nice warm" is what you make of what you have. It is the threshold people pass to hang a hat or a heart or a hollyhock lady.

soul PROJECT

Value Reminiscence

Storytelling is medicine for the soul, and families are the guardians of community and culture. So when we spark memories for each other, even on sensitive topics, we create an environment in which healing may start.

You can inspire others by sharing the historical context of your life and your values, experiences, accumulated life wisdom, and insights. Stories also mend rifts between generations or individuals, because when you honor what was good, you find how to forgive what was bad and reconcile with your past.

Read anew the biblical legacy of this tradition as recorded in Genesis 49.

Create an heirloom document for your loved ones. Whether your personal history is written or passed along orally through a video or cassette tape, your reminiscing is a vital exercise for the spirit. Writing your memoirs, particularly at a turning point, in midlife, or toward the end of a long life, will preserve the most valuable resource you can give your loved ones: the love and wisdom you brought to this world. You'll find joy and surprise, as will others.

Get ready for the adventure, then, and let the following tips guide you in preserving your personal and family pearls.

Gather the strongest memories that lie on the surface of your experience. Listen compassionately to yourself. Jump-start your reflections by bringing to mind

- turning points and defining moments and your emotive responses;
- times you felt strong emotions, ecstasy or despair;

- what you're concerned about or believe;
- what you're grateful for, things you've learned early or late in life;
- family anecdotes, sayings, traditions, and recipes;
- vacation chronicles and journals from trips or birthday parties;
- what your house or hometown looked like and your favorite things about it;
- your favorite books, movies, music, clothes, and places;
- people who influenced you and how they changed you;
- what you will regret not having done if you don't live long enough;
- hopes and dreams for loved ones.

Write or record your memories at random. Start with the most vivid things in your memory or the things that meant the most to you. Work your way to the vaguer memories and then to the very faint. Just record what comes to you and don't stress over what you don't remember. Now thread these together into a treasured work of art. Pen or type them on separate pieces of paper and compile by date, starting furthest back. Attach one to the other by metal clip rings from a stationery store just as they are. You may want to copy the pages and present a chain of them as a gift to family members for a special occasion.

Create a personal time capsule by gathering personal mementos, writing small notes recording what each item means to you, and storing them in an airtight mouse-proof box for safekeeping. Include a love letter to family members you may never meet, such as great-grandchildren or grandnieces and grandnephews, telling them what you would most like them to know about you.

TWO

Romancing
THE HEARTH

Her epithet will be:
The love of words.
The bonds of home and family.
A spirit of adventure.

John F. Kennedy Jr.
(about his mother, Jackie)

n Frank Baum's *The Wizard of Oz*, an angry Dorothy runs away
from home and sets out to find her own way in the world. A
storm suddenly sweeps across the plains. Dorothy runs back but
is unable to get into the storm shelter where others are safe from
an approaching tornado. She enters the old farmhouse just before
it is picked up and hurled through the air. Finally, it plummets
into the strange and colorful land of Oz. Homesick and longing
for what is familiar, Dorothy sets out on an adventure directed

toward finding her way back home to Kansas. In the classic conclusion, Dorothy says, "If I ever go looking for my heart's desire again, I won't look further than my own backyard."

Like Dorothy, I'm searching (at some point, aren't we all?) for the yellow brick road leading me back to where I belong.

Life started out optimistically enough. Being happy and successful seemed fairly simple. But somewhere confusion entered, then doubt. Eventually the pathway forked and led through scary places. Only a sense of purpose and a certain homesickness drove me on. At one point the adventure turned into a nightmare. Terrorized by flying monkeys and haunted by memories of a place where love once embraced me, I was carried somewhere far away from where I started. I despaired of ever getting home again.

A contemporary story with the same theme is based on the true adventure of Jim Lovell: *Apollo 13*. As an astronaut in the NASA space program, Lovell is on the bright pathway to his dream of walking on the moon. Worthy a dream as this is, it is a sidetrack to the precious things in life, yet Lovell doesn't realize this until later. Huddled freezing, exhausted, and frightened after the command module survives an explosion en route, Lovell faces a test much more dramatic than a moon landing. He watches from within as the landing module floats past the spot where they had intended to touch down.

"Beautiful," says his copilot. "Man, we were close."

Lovell turns away, wrestling with his dream of leaving tracks in the moon dust and of gazing at the earth from its surface. Looking beyond the moon, he says to his crew, "Let's go home."

But it is not so simple. The NASA adventure turns into a nightmare. Though feared doomed, the crew does survive and Lovell's commentary at the end of the story is bittersweet. Now gazing at the moon from his own backyard, he muses, "They called us a successful failure. I watched other men walk on the moon from our house in Houston. I sometimes catch myself looking at the moon and at changes of fortune, thinking of all the thousands of people who worked to bring the three of us home."

There's no place like home.

Like Dorothy and Lovell, I found that getting lost was necessary to understand that romance and adventure are waiting for me right where I least expect to find them. But how many of us finally, earnestly recognize that? Some people never do. To recognize the precious things, you must climb over the rainbow and reach farther than the stars. On the deepest level, your innate desire for romance and adventure is in fact a search for the beloved within yourself—not a knight on a white horse or even some awesome achievement. True romance and adventure are not going out into the wide world to find "the one." They are discovering once and for all that you already are the one. They involve coming full circle, home to yourself.

The ancient Hebrew word *nephesh*, translated "soul" in English versions of the Old Testament, actually encompasses the idea of body, soul, and spirit. *Nephesh* implies absolutely that these three aspects of humanity are integrated, a unity. In biblical thought, then, we are made in the image of God, profoundly whole, not bifurcated parts. Our identity can't be split three ways. It is on a physical hearth, our bodies, that we burn the fuel that feeds our souls and spirits. Romancing the hearth of our lives creates synergy among all three parts. It is appropriate then to express our relationship with the Creator not just spiritually but in a material body and in a local context.

I studied this woven interconnection of body, soul, and spirit— and experienced it—during the period when my marriage was ending. At the time it seemed like my home, my local context, was also dissolving. My worries about financial stability and losing my house were fearsome. To complicate the matter, a long siege of emotional starvation had left me dazed. I longed for reciprocal intimacy on many levels. Well-meaning friends reminded me that God's love was ever the same, that he is always present with me. But the mere knowledge of this spiritual reality did little to salve my wounds or help me stake a new claim to personal significance.

I needed to find a physical place to enact the divine romance. We all do. Our entire lives are a search for love—played out in friendships, marriage, families, and the passion with which we pursue our work, as well as prayer and worship. This search is concrete and sensual. It needs a place.

Aberrations of this search for love are obvious in dysfunctional mechanisms that target the body as a place to verify "I exist." Pornography, sexual and alcohol/drug addiction, various methods of body mutilation, and diseases like anorexia are meant to verify that I am real—they affect the flesh. There are many other subtler manifestations of the human search to find a burning hearth. We're hoping to find what has been called the "unbearable lightness of being." But all the time we're looking, the Son of God is hanging on a cross—a physical expression in a particular geographical location—saying, "I love you just the way you are." Upon that material hearth, we find evidence of eternal romance, the kind possible only in oneness of body, soul, and spirit. No wonder human beings crave romance and a particular place to enact it. We host an inherent longing for redemptive love to be woven into our lives—right here on this earth. In bodies we're given a physical space to express who we are, feel emotions, and think ideas. In bodies we're given a habitat—of different sizes and shapes—in which our souls and spirits can dwell and connect with the divine.

"A good woman is worth more than rubies," it has been said, and then the citation links her to her body, her intelligence, her emotions, and her sense of place on this earth: "She does her work with energy. Her arms are strong. She likes to use her mind and works with her hands too. She knows that what she makes and what she does is good. She says, 'Yes! It's good!' And when she looks toward the future, it is so bright it burns her eyes."[1]

It is in our homes and our own backyards that we transcribe who we are—body, soul, spirit—in a visual, literal way. For women, nesting is an intuitive expression of romancing, keeping the fuel burning on the hearth of our lives. A single friend of mine owns a "fly-in" bed-and-breakfast tucked away in the mountains. The inn includes two honeymoon suites, each room with a picturesque name. This friend, who is also a private airplane pilot who is tough and goal oriented, told me unpredictably, "I love romance." Her specialty at the inn is hosting weddings (for which she built a Victorian gazebo) and receptions (for which she decorated the large sitting room). "My inn makes it easy," she says; "the house is the party!"

Isn't that the truth—whether we own a B&B or not? Our homes become the place where we dance to the party of our lives. Or at least we should, shouldn't we?

Look around you. What do you see? A house that needs re-decorating, remodeling, a paint job? A parcel of ground that is too small, too rocky, too bare? Look *harder*. That's what Raffiki says to lost and lonely Simba in *The Lion King*.

"I know what I have to do," Simba replies. But when he finally reaches his own backyard, nothing is as it was. All is burned-out wasteland.

"We're gonna fight for this?" his friend Timone asks.

"Yes, this is my home," Simba answers.

"Well, talk about your fixer-upper!"

Where have your dreams of romance taken you? Beyond? Higher? Or to a tangled place? A lonely place? Even despair?

Look harder. What do you see? A place where everybody knows your name? A place to begin all over again? Do you see *home* when you reenter your own backyard? It is a safe place to fall. It is the place where everything is possible.

Start by doing one thing to enact romance right where you are. Will you light a fire on the hearth or a candle on the windowsill tonight? Will you choose Mozart or James Brown to serenade you and the people you love? Will you employ the scent of roses or freshly baked cookies to revitalize your senses? Your home, like mine, is a physical place to play out the divine romance. Your own backyard is the place to party-on.

Ekaterina Gordeeva, 1988 Olympic gold medalist in pairs ice skating, took a microphone after her first solo performance and spoke to the audience. Six months earlier, her husband and skate partner, Sergei Grinkov, had collapsed during practice and died of a heart attack. In a shy, emotional voice, Ekaterina crossed the arena from side to side, saying with wistful urgency, "Say you love them one more time. Just tell them that you love them. One more time. While you still have the chance."

Ekaterina paid the ultimate price for her lesson about romancing the hearth, then she took the courage and grace to talk about it publicly. She, like Dorothy in Oz and Jim Lovell circling the earth, has been someplace that only a few of us will ever go. What she learned should ring in our ears forever.

soul PROJECT

Make a Testament:
A Picket-Fence Reflection

Mom and Dad brought me home to Maple Street in a shining-with-hope postwar world. The house was my parents' first purchase: $3,000 on a veteran's loan. Daddy built a white picket fence all around it. He had survived D-day and the push into France. Neither crass materialism nor rock 'n' roll had yet appeared on the American scene. But the world was a scary place for a pudgy little girl with frizzy hair and a sensitive soul.

A paw print in the floor of our garage both fascinated and frightened me. Daddy teased that a black bear had ventured by and left his print when the cement was wet. In my three-year-old mind, the bear was still in the neighborhood prowling about and looking for me. Playing in our backyard was not innocent. I hung out close to the back porch or around my mother's ankles in the flower garden, an eye toward the parameters of the picket fence.

Is there a less-than-idyllic situation in your life? What can you do to confront it? What symbol would you use to speak as a testament to your courage? I never did meet the bear on Maple Street, but I've faced many "bears" since I've grown up, and I found them less fearsome than I believed.

Imagined danger or not, life doesn't always feel safe—even in the most idyllic of places and times. No escape from misfortune is guaranteed. I've found, half a century later, that the best way to cope with that fact is to live life fully anyway. I keep an eye out for danger, not in order to avoid it, but to courageously confront it.

THREE

No Copycat
CORRIDOR

Destination rooms get all the attention, but . . . little inconsequential in-between places are often the setting for dramatic moments. Grand entrances and exits. Big hellos, tearful good-byes, door-slamming rows!

Cynthia Rowley and Ilene Rosenzweig

I once lived in a thatched-roof, timbered farmhouse in Denmark, close to the Baltic Sea. Surrounded by a cobbled courtyard, the outside of this house exuded charm. To enter, one had to push open an enormously heavy, hand-carved Dutch door. This felt like entering a fairy tale, and so upon first visit I stepped across the floor of unmortared bricks ready for adventure.

I soon found that anything spilled on those bricks would fall right between the cracks and disappear. I also discovered that the primitive, dark kitchen was a playground for an extended family of mice, some quite stout.

As was the architectural norm in homes of that era, one room led directly into another. From the tiny kitchen, one entered the dining area—large enough to seat a good-sized family and quite a few hired farmhands—and this was adjacent to the formal parlor. A steep, iron spiral staircase led upstairs where one bedroom led into another, and you had to go through the first bedroom, then the second, to get to the only bathroom. In other words, there were no ways to avoid personal quarters or render privacy.

The idea of the corridor, a centrally located hallway with bedrooms and bathrooms opening off from it, wasn't known in Europe until the seventeenth century. Previously families lived with a more generous idea of togetherness. Often more than one family lived beneath one roof and in only one or two rooms. Just a little imagination can conjure a lot of interesting scenarios in homes of two or three hundred years ago. But guessing at how comfortably the families experienced their homes is based on our own culture in which individuality is priority. The invention of the home corridor brought to Europe not just intermediary space but expectations of independence and privacy, part of a raised standard of living.

Today each family member seems to take for granted the right to a room of his or her own and a corridor by which to access it. We guard our right to personal space, free of intrusion. Many kids today have their own telephones, televisions, and personal computers in their bedrooms. The latest custom homes equip each bedroom with its own bathroom as well; master suites may have two full bathrooms. Such homes are, in fact, lavish palaces replete with suites that make it possible to live in isolation.

With architecture facilitating independence and a demand for more space instead of sharing what we have, has the family gained or lost? Is it unreasonable to expect family members to take turns in a single shower? Is it unfair to have to put up with a sibling snoring in the same room or even in the same bed? Has something gone missing?

I wonder.

Apparently I'm not the only one. The 2002 edition of *Frontier House*, produced by Public Broadcasting, followed three families who homesteaded 1880s style in the Montana wilderness. After living four months in a one-room cabin they built themselves, one family returned to their 5,000-square-foot home in Malibu with a dramatic realization. The mother found their California house too big, saying she never knew if anybody else was home. Her daughters complained that they were bored since returning to their affluent lifestyle. They spent most of their time at the mall since there was little else to do. The son claimed that he missed spending time with his father where he was included in the work and where he learned to hunt and fish. The father, back to his corporate job, missed the togetherness of the family sleeping side by side in the cabin loft where there were no walls or corridors to divide them.

It's interesting that the concept of the "family bed" is being revived in the second millennium among young parents. Is it any coincidence that this is happening alongside multiple private quarters and the demise of the "family room"? The now defunct family room implied that family members had to reach a consensus about what to do together. It has been replaced by an open "great room," in which family members may pursue individual pursuits. Today's living quarters, it seems, are about accommodating different lifestyles and schedules. We build our homes for privacy and individuality, then we must invent "new" ideas like the family bed as a way to retrieve old-fashioned feelings of togetherness.

Fingerprints are another old-fashioned thing that was banished in the immaculate modern home. Our homes already have family fingerprints all over them, says author/photographer Mary Randolph Carter, whose classic *American Family Style* captures nostalgic lifestyles. Carter speaks of a spiritual concept that can be expressed on many levels in our homes themselves: cooking, gardening, and entertaining.

Hallways, notorious for family fingerprints, are a case in point. One young mom capitalized on this, helping her kids make handprints all over the corridor walls, each with different colors of paint. Each year she adds a few more with their slightly larger hands or adds the hand of a toddler just joining the display. The hallway in her home has become a collage of family history.

No doubt the corridor is here to stay. Those of us who have lived in college dormitories will never forget late evenings when everybody gathered in the hall to swap gossip or to share funny stories, poetry, class research, notes, or papers. The corridor was a place to reconnect on an intimate level, the way you couldn't connect anywhere else on campus. Doors ajar, rooms with comfy beds and chairs went begging when pajama-clad kids sat cross-legged on the floor just to hang out.

Once my daughters went to college and were enjoying this experience for themselves, I missed the crowded, noisy commotion in our hallway at home. It had become just a dark, quiet place leading to three empty bedrooms. I wondered why, when my kids were small and as energetic as Disney's happy mice, I ever wanted a second-floor master suite away from them. Did I really feel our house was too small? Was I really envious of families in the larger houses on the block? Thank heavens God didn't answer my prayers for a remodel, because I would have languished in even larger empty rooms.

With my girls gone, I decided to reinvent the corridor in my home. I wanted to reframe the idea of "empty nesting," giving it a more positive identity, and create in my home a chic, updated look and feel. I felt fortunate to find a vintage French-paned window with distorted glass that just fit the space between the corridor walls. I added hinges and hung it as an architectural element above the tall opening. Below that, on a closet rod, I hung a curtain of polished striped cotton on oversized wooden rings. That partition contains the heat in my living room and eliminates dark, empty space, no longer used. Since my bedroom opens off the living room, I live again in a room-to-room house, a retro concept that fits my life-without-kids-again style.

It's a style you'll probably never see profiled in *LivingRoom Magazine* or *Chic Simple*. I don't have a shiny chrome kitchen or a garden bathroom. There are no buffer zones "so early risers can avoid disturbing others" as heralded in glowing terms by journalists documenting modern homes. There are no crystal chandeliers hanging from the ceiling or Italian marble on the floors. When *Time* announced, "We don't want our houses to suggest English cottages anymore. Volume has replaced coziness," I answered, "Not at my place." What trend watchers call "overachieving homes" and "the American lust for space" will never be reality for me.[1] Some people say that the only reality is one's perception of reality. If that is true, then I do live in a fairy tale after all.

On weekends or holidays when all three girls are home, we cluster around the fire in too few chairs. Mornings we tiptoe into one room to snuggle together in one bed. Not only are we used to the close proximity; we thrive in it. The conflictive jockeying for space and the forced capitulation to compromise and what seemed like inconvenience have wrought something good in our family. When we were together, we were *together* because the rooms were small and the walls thin, and the bathroom often saw all four of us primping at one time: tangling curling iron cords, using each other's towels, and fighting over whose lipstick was whose.

My kids seem attached to the house they grew up in, and when recently my continued possession of it was threatened, they put their weight strongly on the "keep it" side of the fight. "This is our house too," they said with emotive empathy.

Thousands of miles away from that thatched-roof farm near the Baltic Sea, my home is no Old World fantasy, nor is it a postmodern castle. But it is a shelter baptized with family fingerprints—corridors and all.

soul PROJECT

Hang Out and About Your Hallways

When amplifying the ambience quotient in your home, don't leave out the corridor.

- Light flickering tea candles in glass sconces along the walls at eye level for medieval charm.
- Hang quirky flea market finds from the ceiling on large cup hooks—for example, playful, brightly painted children's chairs or a black hat collection.
- Paint one wall of a favorite room periwinkle blue in spring, then mocha in autumn.
- Fill shelves, installed between ceiling and doors, with books organized by color.
- Apply beaded board halfway up the walls to add a stately Victorian look.
- Hang in an end corner a whimsical object d'art, such as a sprightly painted birdhouse.

- Avoid hanging china plates or breakable wall décor where the bump-and-break factor is high.
- Add a dash of class by hanging a chandelier that you create with crystals and wire and a light core from a builders' supply.
- Involve kids in painting a simple mural you've sketched at their eye level.
- Create a collage of small, decorative mirrors to reflect light from rooms or lighting fixtures.
- Create a message center with blackboard paint on a board or wall, and hang a tin of colorful chalk beside it.
- Display family photographs, but in a noncliché way. Reinvent the hallway family album by playing with color and thematic frames, or go dramatic with all black-and-white images and frames. Another idea: Arrange same-sized pictures in triangles instead of the usual linear lineup. Or use coordinating decorating ribbon to link picture backs together in a playful display. One more: Hang tiny wall vases or sconces between or around the photographs.
- Feature a collage of framed photos composed in ten easy steps:
  1. Measure the width, length, and depth of your wall area where the pictures will be hung, just above eye level.
  2. Mark out an area equivalent in size and shape on the floor using a newspaper as a template.
  3. Move your pictures around on the newspaper, trying different positions until striking "the look."
  4. Measure your pictures and the spaces using consistent spacing; note measurements.
  5. Miniaturize your plan on a separate piece of paper for reference when hanging.
  6. Making horizontal and vertical lines straight, pull wire taut on back of each picture.
  7. Measure from the wire to the center top of frame; note measurements; allow for this distance when hanging.

8. Mark picture and spacing measurements on wall, starting top left, with light pencil marks.
9. Use measurements noted in step 4 to align picture hooks; hammer gently into place.
10. Hang pictures in the same order as on miniature template.

FOUR

Back Doors to
BLUE-JEAN DAYS

In the days when the children were there to come back from school, they brought the world back with them. They brought tales of their adventures back with them to me whose only adventures most days had taken place inside my head. As surely as they brought back homework, they brought back home to that house, brought back more than anything else themselves to that house.

Frederick Buechner

Since the milkman stopped making deliveries to the back doors of America, it appears that the idea of an intriguing rear entrance has fallen into oblivion. As I browse through home and garden magazines looking for a photograph of at least one traditional back door—like the one 1950s sitcom character the Beaver walked through after school to find milk and cookies every day—I find few apart from marketing ads. Why is it that back doors elude us today?

As an adjective, *backdoor* means "indirect, concealed, or devious." If the shoe fits, we must wear it, I suppose, because the back door is usually the one leading into the garage. It's the portal through which you pass to bring in the groceries, hurry kids into the car for school, or find the recycle bin. The garage acts as a buffer zone between the back door and the world. No one but family enters or exits this way, and for Generation X and their children, the image of back door carries no nostalgic overtones because it is shrouded in darkness.

Of course, the idea of back door has, like everything else, continued to evolve. In fact, if your house was built in the last twenty to thirty years, you probably have several back doors: sliding glass or French doors onto a patio or deck, an exit from the master bedroom or one to the side of the house leading to an RV pad or storage shed. Any one or all of these doors, say practitioners of the ancient art of placement, represent indirect opportunity. If that is true, then I suppose the more doors the merrier. But let's think about that.

I recently spent the night alone in my parents' new two-story house. Besides the front door and the back door to the garage, the house has no less than four other rear doors. Being there overnight, I was spooked with all those doors to lock after dark. Returning to my one-story cottage with its single back door was a relief.

I've never imagined anything threatening walking through my back door, but to anticipate *opportunity* walking through the back door and into my life is a new concept. In temperate weather I leave the back door ajar so my dog can come and go. Occasionally a mouse has slipped in and once a squirrel. But no one ever delivers a package there or knocks with an inquiry or invitation. Long gone are the days of kids running in and out to play. The rear threshold is now used to fetch firewood in winter and to turn on sprinklers in summer. Where is opportunity in that?

We take the back door for granted because it is usually not dressed up or swept clean for company. At times we go to our back doors wrapped in nothing but a towel—to call in the cat or gauge the temperature—when we would never appear at our front door that way. We keep unsightly stuff there, just temporarily, of course, but doesn't it usually sit there longer than planned? After all, it's just the back door; a rather ho-hum kind of place. You wouldn't assign its activity much significance. Yet isn't it through the back doors of our lives that the real stuff comes and goes?

In my childhood home, it was through the back door that Dad appeared after work. On its cement stoop, Mother served peanut-butter sandwiches after Saturday's *Hopalong Cassidy* show. Through that same door, two little girls in patent leather shoes exited with their family for the First Baptist Church twice each Sunday.

I'd say this is a heap-big helping of significance. How much have we missed by not welcoming more through the back doors of our lives? We hurry our children through them to a hundred activities each year, but do we listen to what kids say as we grab the gear and go? How often do we delight in their animated personalities in the process? You and I provide food and clothing for our families, loading it by the sackful into our kitchens, disposing of the packaging in huge garbage containers outside the back door. All this hustle and bustle is inevitable in raising a family, but how often do we perceive it as opportunity?

Next time you use any one of your multiple back doors, think about the reasons for the traffic in and out. If you have children or pets and creatures you tend at home, you may experience more chaos than serenity through your back door. Embrace it. Be thankful.

A back door is like comfort food or a pair of faded jeans. My back door screen gets ripped, and I let it be. The rickety steps below it will probably never be fixed. The thin line of white paint I dribbled across the window pane two years ago still smiles at me. Aside from an occasional bird hitting the glass to fall dazed on the deck, not much unexpected happens there. But on my grandparents' farm, the back door was always used as the front door. It faced the chicken coop, the grain barn, the windmill, the machinery sheds, and the yard where Grandpa built a merry-go-round for his grandkids. It was outside this "back" door that homemade ice cream was cranked every summer Sunday afternoon. And just as soon as our 1954 Studebaker pulled into the driveway, Grandma appeared there smelling of wheat fields and lilac water.

When my grandparents Leah and Jesse retired in town, their bungalow was literally on Main Street, USA. Their one back door led to an unfenced backyard. I guess the world was safer then. I know it was simpler; this, in spite of the fact our grandmothers lugged tons of laundry to public Laundromats and home again, only to hang it all on a line—where else?—just outside the back door. Back doors sounded like sheets flapping in the wind or neighbors swapping gossip. They felt like wind in your face as you fetched clanking milk bottles just before dawn.

I wonder what my own children will remember of the back doors in their lives. Will they recall a sandbox filled with toy dishes and naked dollies? What sounds will bring back memories of snowball fights or hide-and-seek in the twilight? Will a back door call to mind the smell of hamburgers cooked on a humble hibachi? Will the howl of coyotes in the distance remind them of mother-daughter slumber parties under the stars, and their quibble over who was going to sleep closest to the back door? How many times have I watched deer families grazing on our grass and called the girls to "Look, look out the back door"? How many shoe-box burials did Leyah perform in the bird-mole-hamster cemetery just beyond it?

Have you ever stopped to wonder about everything your back door has experienced? We all have our homemade rituals there, but we usually don't consider them anything special. I think my back door would tell about how year after year I secured it last thing before going to bed. The lock was broken, so I improvised by placing a cut-to-fit broom handle into the sliding space. I was locking in the precious things, like babies, toddlers, schoolkids, and warmth; and beautiful things too: the poem book written by my grandmother, the antique lamp salvaged from an abandoned farm, the vase potted by a local artist. I was locking in a secure family identity in the form of irreplaceable documents, records, and personal files.

And what was I locking out? The cold. Critters in the dark. Potential violation of my family and my person. Vandalism of our home. The act of locking up each night is motivated by much more than fear or precaution. The story my back door tells gives me a different perspective on life in its fullness. When I lock up each night, I'm not worrying about how much I had to pay for a new windshield that day or how much I have to do the next day. Locking the back door at night is a way to say good night to the moon, and beneath it, to my habitat on this earth.

Tonight, after locking up as usual, I will turn back to the hub of my home and remember how I once would go tuck covers around sleeping children or answer a last call for a drink of water. Tonight I will switch off the music, close the damper on the woodstove, and put out the last burning candle. I will think about how my back door is an icon representing indirect opportunity and, if nothing more, a sign to love each day I'm given.

soul PROJECT

Tell Your
Backdoor Story

Get yourself a cup of java or green tea, put on your blue jeans, and pull up a chair in the whereabouts of your back door. Bring with you a notebook or paper and pen. Recollect the activity around your back door. Who goes in and out there? Where are they or you going? What kind of gear is dragged back and forth? What is the prevailing mood of the people who traverse this portal of your home?

- *Paint with words what you see.* Write stream-of-consciousness style. Note colors: the color of the door, your family members' eyes, their clothing, the stuff going in and out.
- *Write what you hear:* chatter, footsteps of boots or silence of sneakers, the car running outside, birds singing on a spring morning. How do you feel when you think about the comings and goings of your back door? Write in a rambling kind of way that notes all the details you can recall through the years you've lived in your house.
- *Tell this story from your door's point of view.* What does your door remember? Simple, daily routine? Big dramatic moments? Shouting? Whispers? What is the best thing your back door has ever experienced? Who is it thinking of when it reflects over months of events and the passing of seasons?
- *Jot down memories of your childhood doors.* What were the best experiences there? What were the worst? Think in terms of pictures in your mind and jot down the details. Fold all of this up in an envelope and label it to place in your journal later.

FIVE

Windows
SOMETIMES BREAK

Poetry often enters through the window of irrelevance.

M. C. Richards

J ust as eyes are windows to your soul, windows are the eyes of your home. Windows are the contact point for everything housed within; when full of light, they tell other people that you're at home. They reveal character that is dynamic, changing, and alive.

Home décor magazines are full of photographs of windows— as background or as the focal point. Always the windows are metaphor, signifying a whole lot more than openings in the walls of your dwelling.

I don't remember when it started, but long before photography of quaint windows became trendy, I was enchanted by the idea of windows as archetype. Perhaps my intrigue started during travels after college when I lived in many different places, enjoyed and endured many different views, and was forced to put up with many kinds of functional (and often not) windows.

Working in Essex, England, for instance, my view from the second story of a manor house turned institution looked out upon grounds with walls and ponds and chestnut trees. In Århus, Denmark, the arched window in a Victorian-era factory that had been turned into an apartment looked out on the brick wall of a dismal disco below. In the tiny village of Grossgmain, Austria, my window from the third story of the bed-and-breakfast where I worked looked toward the Untesberg—the mountain where Julie Andrews, as Maria, danced and whirled during the opening scene in *The Sound of Music*.

Yes, I've viewed the world through many other windows in exotic places, including a basement window where I could see only feet, each clad in different kinds of shoes, walking down Jerusalem's Street of the Prophets. And ever since, windows have symbolized to me the transparency of women's lives. Windows reveal, most importantly to ourselves, what we're all about under the masks we wear.

I once wrote a column called "An Open Window" for a women's magazine as a way of communicating that I wanted my life to be open to the readers. Nevertheless, I can come across as opaque. A former neighbor recently made this clear. After an exchange of "How are you?" she laughed and made the unexpected comment, "Marlee, there's always so much mystery around you." I realized I sometimes project an image of veiled persona. I'm due for an architectural change, not just refurbished drapery.

At home a window motif is my metaphor to risk openness: A specially installed antique door with a flawed glass window leads to my bedroom. A crumbly paned barn window (found in the forest) hangs as a partition between the kitchen and living area.

My coffee table is a new-to-look-old glass window top where I serve guests, spread out projects, and on occasion prop up my feet. Most significant, perhaps, is my twelve-paned bedroom window installed in the front wall when remodeling the room from a garage. The lower left-hand pane was broken when my ex-husband was moving a large mirror shortly before he left our home. The mirror shattered. As for the broken pane, I never had it replaced, because after our divorce I never had an extra fifty bucks. Yet I've thought a lot about that smashed windowpane with its spiderweb appearance. It became a symbol of our broken home, and I was forced to come to terms with its cold, sharp edges and tacky appearance. Perhaps I never had the window fixed because somehow I knew things need time to be what they are.

Are there shattered windows in your home? Debilitating or chronic illness? Financial ruin? Infertility? A wayward child? An untimely death? Alzheimer's disease? If you live in a house with a broken window like I do, and you can't change the way things are, how about looking through it in a brand-new way?

During my first month of being single again, I hung every picture or photograph throughout my house upside down. It was a quirky way to remind myself not to be in denial but to acknowledge and make peace with the losses. It became a fun way—when visitors came—to take the whole matter lightly.

Windows may not be fixed right away, but that does not mean they will never be mended. Everything may not become clear in a twinkling. It takes courage to begin to think in different ways about anything that gives you pain. It takes courage to see the possibilities in disability or disease or divorce. But that doesn't mean that you and I can't live with style, dignity, and intention.

When my friend Jane moved to town, she bought a fixer-upper with odd and disharmonious character. She'll tell you that had she been able to afford a house needing less work, she wouldn't have purchased it. The quirky elements attracted her to the clunky cottage. Jane's dining room window looks at a cement wall—one foot away—the wall of what she sympathetically calls the "Woe-Be-Gone." But when she revealed just a few of her many ideas to turn that homely view into an appealing vista, I was envious of her ability to envision the impossible. She transcended the unlikely, not by trying to cover it up or make it something it was not, but by using the blank wall to advantage. Now it showcases a classy folk art sculpture that complements her dining room motif.

Wherever you live, even temporarily or on vacation, capture the view from each of your windows in a photograph. In beautiful cities like Paris or Manhattan, or along a boring stretch of highway, train your eye to see the unexpected and the charming. Look closer. Do you see a tiny flower or blade of grass shooting up through asphalt? Is that a child's face in the distance? A gum wrapper tangled in the weeds? Are you enough of a poet to see the art in seeming irrelevance?

If nothing else, snap a shot of your hand, foot, or face against the windowpane. Go with the view you've been given and capture memories that grow insight about what I call "the bad boys" of life: ugly views or cracked windowpanes. It's all about changing your lens. Cameras that come with an assortment of lenses can be used to create a new way of seeing. If your hotel room view does not face the Spanish Steps or the Eiffel Tower, then twist on a different lens and look at what you do see in a different way.

This is what it means to have soul and to open windows to the soul.

I've stayed in a lot of funky places at home and abroad because I travel on a budget. I'm usually scrimping my way through wherever, and I'm good at making do—or as I prefer to think of it, "daring do." While living in a basement hostel in Jerusalem, I watched feet going by through a window to the street above and uncovered a wealth of fodder for stories about people whose faces I never saw. These were stories of cripples and athletes, rich and poor, young and old told by the shoes they wore.

Other stories were inspired by a trip with ten-year-old Lissa in our dependable old Dodge sedan along the coast on northern California's Highway 101. Sleeping side by side on a lopsided air mattress in a simple tent with a window flap that opened to the stars, we listened to the roll of the surf and the crackle of campfires those June nights. We were far from home on a spontaneous journey, and we will always treasure the magic of adventure gained through that window in time.

Years later I stayed in a small-town youth hostel while Lissa attended a college preview weekend. Her friend's mother dropped me off across the tracks, then checked into a glamorous top-floor room in an art deco hotel downtown. The contrast was as glaring as the personal economics of our lives. The dorm-room windows where I stayed were rotted and mildewed. The bathroom locks were broken; the kitchen was cluttered and sparse.

But inside the weathered shell of this wreck of a place, I met the most amazing people—people with nothing but soul, the kind of people who charm me most. A colorful World War II vet claimed to have been the officer to order the action for the story filmed as *Saving Private Ryan* on the French front. He had documentation to prove it. A middle-aged woman, realizing how short life is, and how much she still had to give after her mother died, was living there while working on a master's degree. A young German student wandering through America was gathering stories from the four corners of our country.

How much I might have missed from loftier windows, especially the truth I learned in that dusty dorm in Jerusalem—that it doesn't matter what kind of windows you have, but how you discern what's given you to see.

When I was processing divorce, I eventually let go of the image of broken anything. I made the most of the eleven intact panes in my bedroom window and the other areas of my personhood. I found myself dancing, loving, crying, breathing, moving, and imagining more to come through the windows of my home. The party went on! The transparent woman I wanted to become was not only still within reach but was walking about with more clarity than ever. Little by little the light began to shine through the windows of my home and life again.

Several leaded prisms in the shape of hearts now hang in the window at my desk. They disperse color from the southwest sun back into my room and splash it across the opposite wall. Through the prism of what only appears to be broken—non-parallel planes—light is more widely dispersed. Colors show up that would not have otherwise.

Today I can say and mean it that I do not want to be an over-dressed window who, like an overdressed woman, does not trust her intrinsic beauty. What about you? Stop and gaze through your windows. What do you see? Even a shattered window has a view. A potentially negative event can be transformed into something that propels you in a positive direction.

The week I had dreaded for years, when my youngest daughter left home for college, I planned a cathartic event designed to celebrate my identity as other than that defined primarily by motherhood. I legally changed my last name from that of my children's father. I used my new name for the first time that same week to sign mortgage documents making me the owner of the home where I had raised our children.

Since then I've been celebrating that reality by painting trim that was once raw wood now a beautiful pearly white.

I guess it's time the broken windowpane is replaced too.

soul PROJECT

Find Your Window to the Soul

R eflect on the different shapes of windows you've seen in any building or magazine, cathedral or cottage. Which style speaks to your sensibilities? Have windows ever been the subject of a recurring or particularly vivid dream?

Dreaming of windows often means release of restrictions or getting away from problems. Cut out pictures from brochures or magazines of appealing windows and glue them in a small notebook or journal. Call this your *House-a-Home Journal*. Research online the shape or structure of windows that appeal to you or appear on the fringes of your consciousness. What can you learn about yourself? Document ideas that come to mind as I did below.

A vivid dream I remember: On a sightseeing tour in an old cobblestoned city, I entered a building and went down to the basement. At the end of a labyrinthlike, one-way corridor, I came to a small alcove. In front of me was a small triangular-shaped window just large enough to crawl through. The wings of the window pushed open from the middle. A woman in front of me crawled through wearing a business suit. I was next in line but couldn't get the window to stay open while hoisting myself up and pulling myself through. I tried and tried, watching as the lady in front of me hurried down a deserted street and disappeared. Feeling trapped, I began to panic. By continually attempting to get out, I finally pulled myself through into the daylight.

My reflections on this: The labyrinth represents the birth canal, and the triangle-shaped window represents the birth opening that seemed too small. My trying to emerge was my attempt to release personal restrictions holding me back from a midlife rebirth. I believe my dream is telling me to keep trying because something new wants to be born in me.

SIX

Walls
HAVE EARS

See, I have inscribed you on the palms of My hands;
Your walls are continually before Me.

Isaiah 49:16

Ten years ago, with five people living in 1,000 square feet
of space and only one bathroom, I began to dream of an
addition to our house. Since there was no dining room,
our table was squeezed between the galley-style kitchen and the
laundry area, adjacent to the back door. I longed for a room large
enough to put a leaf in our table for guests and for an additional
bedroom with bath away from the cramped corridor.

I began to whisper about my dreams, telling God just what I
wanted. "Please, Lord," I prayed, "enlarge our borders."

That's when I began to realize the walls were listening too.

God answered, "Enlarge the place of your tent, . . . stretch out the curtains of your dwellings; do not spare; lengthen your cords, and strengthen your stakes."[1]

Much to my surprise, God was making *me* fully accountable for the expansion I desired. This would begin a process through which I began to grow spiritually, in tach with my house. I began to realize that I am supported by my home's walls in more than a physical way. By cooperating with the dynamic of God's kingdom, as I ever take the next step toward it, my home symbolizes true sanctuary; its very walls are imbued with spiritual sensibilities as places of refuge and protection.

Jewish people have known this for ages, observes architectural and design author Laura Cerwinske. Since the destruction of the second temple in AD 79, the Jewish people have been sustained by the holiness of the family rather than the holiness of a particular building, she says. The notion of the temple housing "the original altar of sacrifices . . . was transmogrified as the dining table of every Jewish home. . . . With the realization that worship exists wherever the soul seeks communion, we recognize that the true sanctuary is of our own making."[2]

In my finite mind, adding onto and remodeling my house was an issue of money and of my making that money. But in eternal terms, the kingdom paradigm, the issue wasn't finances—it was faith.

With no cash to fulfill my home-as-sanctuary desires, I began merely to imagine them. That is the first step, even the poets know. "Nothing, without first a dream," Carl Sandburg wrote.

Then I began to make imagination concrete. I drew the dimensions of proposed new walls—first on paper and then in the dusty earth to the rear of our kitchen window. Rocks the size of softballs became my pencils as I lay stone after stone to show the walls of a large dining area off the kitchen wall of our home.

To the north our single-car garage would be transformed ⸏ bedroom, and I laid additional rocks in the earth where I imagined an adjoining bathroom and walk-in closet. At each corner I made little altars of pebbles. In this unpretentious ritual, imagination slowly became faith.

Daily I'd rethink the shape or size and stand inside the rock "walls" envisioning our family gathered there. Grace seemed content to let the dream incubate. Carried by the momentum, step by step, I walked to the edge of all I knew—and then took one step more. I called contractors, compared estimates, calculated bank costs, and researched their various financing options. Timing allowed us a miracle. Interest rates dropped, and although my income didn't increase, my courage to refinance the house did. Somehow in this process new walls went up.

Now I see that once I was ready to act, to apply for a loan, and see what could happen, the concept of refinancing coincided with lower interest rates and made it possible. I also understand that if I had not begun to take specific steps, refinancing at the best rates would not have done any good.

On occasion I run into the builder who raised these walls, expanding our house by 700 square feet. He no longer greets me with a jovial inquiry about whether the walls are still standing. After numerous erratic mountain windstorms and ferocious icy winters, it is me who states, "The walls are standing. The walls are strong."

After all I've read in the Bible about how the survival of ancient cities depended on strong walls, the strength of walls has meant something to me. The idea was reinforced when as a twenty-something living in Jerusalem I walked around the walls of the Old City, the same walls Nehemiah prayed over. I journaled daily atop the walls at the Golden Gate looking toward the Mount of Olives. I explored David's citadel above a maze of narrow meandering streets where Arab traders still buy and sell in ancient tradition. Into the crevices of the Western Wall, the holiest site of the Hebrews, I, as pilgrims have done for centuries, stuck prayers written on small notes.

Twenty-five years after these youthful ventures, I returned to Jerusalem to find excavations alongside and under the Western Wall in the old city. These led down to a paved street built during Roman occupation. Visitors are taken deep into an underground tunnel and eventually reach a place where the wall, lit only by candlelight, becomes damp. This section of the wall is believed to be closest to where the temple once stood on the opposite side, where now stands the Islamic holy of holies, the beautiful mosque called Dome of the Rock. At this very spot, water seeps from the face of the stone in the Western Wall. Since there is no known water source on the other side, the strange occurrence is accepted as a mystery. Some Jews will tell you the wall is weeping—weeping over the desecration of the temple. Near this continual dripping, thousands of scraps of paper rolled into tiny wads are tucked into crevices, documenting the intimate prayers of many people over great periods of time.

The truth is, wherever we live the walls hold our prayers. Walls always observe the history of place. They embrace war and peace, changes of all kinds, our love, and our fears. When we paint or decorate the walls of our homes, we do more than refurbish a room or make it look pretty. In some way we perform ritual of the most profound nature.

The walls of my house are built with three-by-six boards instead of the usual two-by-fours. Sturdy and stout, these walls have listened to my children's prayers. Armchair mystic that I am, I believe the prayers of my children have become ensconced in the corners and crevices of their rooms and have made our home sacred space on earth.

Novelist Sue Monk Kidd gets at this in *The Secret Life of Bees*, in which Lily listens to the bees who live in the walls of her room. Lily says, "I imagined them in there turning the walls into honeycombs, with honey seeping out for me to taste. . . . Despite everything that happened that summer, I remain tender toward the bees."[3] It is as if the bees themselves perform the ritual blessing.

As a reader, I am left to ponder the symbolic meaning of life that goes on in the walls of the houses that hold us and silently wait for us to listen back with tenderness. I wonder what the walls of your home communicate about you, and I wonder if all our walls are really just backdrops for the silhouettes of our lives.

When I think of "silhouettes," I think of those Victorian silhouette pictures framed in metal with bubble glass that depict couples involved in elegant activities like dancing or riding in a horse and buggy. Wouldn't it be an intriguing twist if all of our family moments were being preserved as shadow pictures on the walls of our homes?

When the atomic bomb dropped on Hiroshima and Nagasaki in August 1945, the shadows of objects and humans were cast permanently on walls by the radiation. If your home life were to become a permanent silhouette in a dramatic, show-stopping moment, what would the shadow picture look like? Would you want to make any changes?

I'm sitting within my walls today, warmed by the heat from the woodstove and pondering these questions for myself. When my family dwindled at two-year intervals from five to four, then three, then two, then one, it was like an earthquake followed by a series of aftershocks. Shortly before my youngest left home, I began putting up baby and childhood pictures of her and her sisters on the walls. I needed to be reminded that an awful lot of warm family happenings took place here. Shadow pictures of raising three children have surely been burned permanently onto the walls of my psyche. I just wanted to see them in color again.

I wonder now what pictures will replace this family motif and motivate me to move ahead to the next big thing.

As our lives change, so do the spaces we live in, says designer Sheila Bridges. In her book, *Furnishing Forward*, she encourages designing and decorating our homes so that they are completely in sync with these life changes.[4]

The walls of my home have been white for years, but last year a friend talked me into colorizing one of them for a change of pace. After much resistance, and when I was guaranteed all could be painted white again, I finally settled on terra-cotta, a favorite color. The difference a new wash of color made in my room, and on my outlook, startled me. From the moment the first stroke was applied, accenting the taupe-colored rock of the hearth, I recognized that walls are sacred backdrops to our homes. Better put, walls are backdrops to our sacred lives. It is appropriate and inevitable that changes in our lives be projected on them and documented in a variety of new ways and new looks.

Each time I've moved from a home, I've prayed for a graced presence to remain there. I believe such a presence lives on somehow in the walls, like honeycomb for the next occupants. As I move on, I'm certain I'll come up against a number of walls. Perhaps I'll hit a few of them going full speed and be knocked out cold. But I'm reminded that Jesus walked through more than a few. When Jesus' disciples met in fear behind locked doors after his resurrection, he transcended the problem of the locked doors and simply appeared in their midst. The same thing happened again eight days later. "And there are also many other things that Jesus did," says the text of John's Gospel.[5]

When walls seem like obstacles to what I want, I need to stop and ask what Jesus would do. His understanding of matters is complete and profound, but just before he ascended to heaven, he declared that even in our imperfect understanding we are to be witnesses of him. Surely the walls of our homes serve not only to protect and enclose us but to allow us to transcend the visible and material world as witnesses of God's grace and power. Every time I step to stretch out the curtains of my dwelling and lengthen my cords, sparing not, God is with me—and the walls are listening.

soul PROJECT

If Your Walls Could Talk . . .

If your walls could talk, what would they say? Create tangible ways to remind family that the daily course of life matters greatly at home. Although most of us don't have time for the elaborate detail that the popular art of scrapbooking demands, we can take shortcuts to documenting love and laughter.

- *Revolve family and friend photos* from camera to refrigerator to the file box every couple of months. Keep the display areas in your home (the fridge, a mirror)—like your lives—fresh and ever changing.
- *Think in themes.* Buy a photo file box or use shoe boxes for each member of the family or divide a single box into seasons, holidays, or family events. Make copies of certain photos to place in themed files that overlap. Add newspaper clippings and other memorabilia (e.g., ticket stubs or award certificates) to the files.

- *Feed souls with memories*—let children you love make place mats with photographs by gluing them in a collage on plastic mats then laminating them. Create special ones for birthdays or school awards.
- *Take snapshots of guests as an alternative guest book,* logging their names and the date they visited.
- *Be ready in a snap to capture your family on film.* Keep a disposable camera in the glove compartment of your car, one in a kitchen drawer, another in a niche by the back door or in a jacket pocket. Send one with your child to school on her birthday or the day of a special assembly.
- *Laugh a little more.* Save bad or cast-off photos in a separate file for kids to make joke cards and silly collages on a rainy day. Cut the photos apart and put them back together in funny ways. Stick labels with silly sayings (available in photo stores) onto the photos.
- *Create stationery with a photo of the recipient* scanned onto paper with a quote and contact information (your children will love this sort of personalized way to connect to their home!).

SEVEN

Not Your Granny's
NOOKS AND CRANNIES

What I have only come to realize is that asking to be delivered to
my passion is the only thing worth praying for.

Sarah Ban Breathnach

The homes in actress Debby Boone's Burbank, California,
neighborhood are small and plain. Economy Chevys and
Fords line the curbs. There are no BMWs, lush gardens,
turquoise pools, or multistory houses.

Then you see it, squeezed between two simple ranch-style
dwellings: a stunning chateau. A river-rock turret rises upward,
swirled like a licorice vine between strands of red brick. Under
a sloped roof are two beautiful stained-glass windows. A cherub
with a broken wing kneels with its back at the front door.

When I arrived to interview Boone on assignment, she led me
right into her kitchen. I couldn't help thinking how deliciously
lived in it was. Layers of whimsical children's art, life-sized paper

dolls, and funky decorations covered every inch of wall space. Boone told me that while house hunting for this home she had hoped to find space for her husband's art projects and to raise their four children. Secretly, she hoped also for a certain amount of charm—within their price range. To prove she found just that, she later took me to the master bathroom. Pulling open a tiny door in the ceiling, she folded out a ladder that led to a small attic. All it needed, she said, was a skylight and—presto!—it could become husband Gabriel's art studio. But that wasn't all.

Boone's house is full of Old World flair, including more than a fair share of nooks and crannies in odd and unused areas. When she toured the house the first time, she couldn't find the stained-glass bay window that looked so pretty from the outside. It wasn't until the Realtor took her through the U-shaped closet off the master bedroom that she spied unexpected sunshine spilling onto the floor between racks of clothes.

Suddenly she knew—this was *the* house.

Once Boone's family moved in, that three-by-three-foot bay window alcove, with its carpeted platform and walls covered in sunshine, became her personal chapel. "I literally go into my closet to pray like Jesus asked us to do in Matthew," she said. "From the window I look onto the street with passing cars and people muted by the pink and green glass. The view reminds me there is a world beyond my place, and I also belong to that world."[1]

I couldn't help wishing for a prayer niche as ambient as Debby Boone's when I returned home from my visit with her. But almost no houses built in the last fifty years have anything like our grannies' nooks and crannies. To re-create the charm of older homes, we have to add to them ourselves, inspired by alcoves we have known from other times and places. Sheltered, inviting, holding our special books and precious objects, such intimate spaces create a natural refuge.

One alcove I remember was the staircase in Grandma and Pa Smith's farmhouse. It was narrow, steep, and cold, taking a sharp left turn toward the second story, after which the stairs seemed to go on forever. As a little girl, I liked sitting on that one angled step and imagining my father as a little boy in flannel pj's climbing those same stairs every night for bed.

In my own childhood home, a tunnel-like closet connected my parents' bedroom to the one I shared with my sister. The closet was great for hide-and-seek or stashing secret treasures among boxes of who-knows-what. It was popular with little friends who came to play. Scrambling through the dresses and shoes with a playmate was like exploring Tom Sawyer's cave or the tombs of the pharaohs.

My Grandmother Daisy's cherry wood, cedar-lined trunk was another childhood nook that held mystery for me. It always stood at the end of her bed in her basement apartment holding the few material keepsakes of her long life—elegant turn-of-the-century feathered hats and flapper dresses with matching beaded bags. The contents have disappeared, but the trunk itself has become a prized possession, now used for storing my own collection of costumes from around the world. It also holds several lengths of filmy, lacy fabrics I plan to sew into artsy pillows someday. The trunk is a niche for memories and dreams alike.

I wished for nooks and crannies for my own children once they came along, but the closest they knew were antique armoires, among the most necessary pieces of furniture for people of past centuries. These were large cupboards for hanging clothes and storing linens that often had intriguing details inside—sometimes cubbyholes or false backs for hiding valuables. It was through one of these that C. S. Lewis's characters entered the world of Narnia in *The Lion, the Witch, and the Wardrobe*; perhaps my girls imagined Lewis's stories better for the large armoire in our home that always held paper and art supplies, books, and stacks of magazines.

Niche is one of my favorite words, not only because it fits neatly on the tip of my tongue, but because I love what it implies. *Have you found your niche in life? Do you market your services or a product to a particular niche?*

One delightful niche for me is that one stair "in the middle of the stairs" that appears in the lovely poem "Halfway Down" by A. A. Milne:

> I'm not at the bottom,
> I'm not at the top;
> So this is the stair
> Where I always stop.[2]

This Christopher Robin kind of niche is much like the flat rock in the sun under the aspen trees in front of my house. Or like the shady spot on the back porch where I take a glass of iced tea on scorching days. It is like my bed where I pray and journal or go to cry. *Niche* in the truest sense is the most private of places. It may be anywhere you go when you want to be alone.

When designing her home, my artist friend Abby Merickel included self-designed mosaic tile around her bathtub in nuances of green. This is the place she goes for time-out and some rejuvenation from her two rambunctious boys. It is a place to simply relax, rest, and find renewal. "That's what I do for fun on the weekend," she laughs, "because I don't have a life!" Or maybe Abby knows that rest in a niche is simply a necessity of life, that it is essential for each of us to find a safe place to curl up once in a while. And if we cannot find that place, we can create it—an alcove, a corner, some crevice where we revert to a womblike simplicity and reconnect with our spirit.

An alcove is a place to reinvest in ourselves: to linger, to be spiritually fertile, to be renewed. But why should something so important and big be confined to places so small? Why not have an entire room set aside for prayer and meditation?

Imagine a room in your house carefully decorated with beautiful things, objects symbolizing the sacred to you. Now add soft lighting and at least one comfortable chair. Such a room inspires faith and facilitates peace. Rooms used specifically for creative purposes are closely related. Imagine a place in your home where you can spread out materials and leave them there to be untouched until you can return to the project on the spur of a moment. Imagine a meditation room or studio that's visual rather than cerebral—the places where Christopher Lowell's "Seven Layers of Decorating" will never reach.

These are centers of serenity where you find the passion to remake the world in spite of overwhelming odds. To retreat into an alcove, a niche, a chamber, or a closet for the purpose of facing fears and foibles is essential. We lay our issues before the Almighty and leave believing in a better outcome. Aren't we changed in positive ways? Every closet may not hold the ambience of the bay window at which Debby Boone prays and studies the Word of God. But even the hard floor of a cellar, when we press close to his heart, is a place for divine appointment. The desire to be at times cloistered, concealed, or clandestine is a part of human nature. And like a girl or boy building a hideaway, we each need to find a personal way to sequester ourselves for a time away from the skeptical world.

Charles Dickens's novels are full of idyllic getaways. And who could forget the attic in which the March girls practiced their own original plays in Louisa May Alcott's *Little Women*? The alcove where I hide most often is the shower. It's in the rush of hot water that I find my soul after a siege of stress or insufficient sleep or the overstimulation of a technical world. Liberal servings of quiet and privacy are offered by the fiberglass walls of the cubicle where I wash the weight of the world away. I find tranquillity and the story my soul is aching to tell me. Mind and emotion reunite in a body that welcomes them like guests at high tea. Take up the search and shape yourself an alcove. You may find your place on a rustic garden bench or in a dormer window under the eaves. Everybody needs one small place of enchantment.

Houses, or in particular our homes, are the scene of experience where human and divine fellowship intersect. The stages in our lives are marked out by where we have lived, by the details of what those places looked like, smelled like, and felt like as we moved from room to room, coming and going with the cares and joys of the world. The places we have lived mark our soul, and as a return on that investment, by living soulfully we transform houses into homes. Sans remodeling, decorating, and new furniture, a house becomes home as we explore its nooks and crannies.

*soul*PROJECT

Make Some Shoestring Elegance

L ife on a shoestring is challenging, engaging, and creative. Why not make it fun? If you like to explore and have plenty of decorating savvy, you'll opt for the bargain table, tag sale, or thrift store first. Keep these tips in mind:

* *Always ask if you can have slightly damaged goods at an additional discount.* You can paint, repair, or hide the flaw in a creative way.

- *Get an artsy one-of-a-kind look by determining to see everything with new eyes.* When shopping for clothes at tag sales or thrift stores, look for items that can be cut apart and sewn together in creative ways.
- *Go for the thrill of a treasure hunt.* Give up preconceived ideas of what you're looking for. Stop at what grabs you: color, texture, style, fabric pattern, odd buttons, weathered leathers.
- *Sort through lots of trash to find a jewel*—and that's what makes it fun. I found a gorgeous jewel-toned Chinese coat two sizes too small. It became a snazzy bedroom wall hanging.
- *Remember last year's trends become tomorrow's children's costumes with a little trim or alteration and imagination.* Last decade's trends can become tomorrow's stylin' clothes for teenagers too.
- *Keep your eyes peeled for unusual décor possibilities:* Mounted deer antlers can be used as a hat rack, worn-out boots make cute planters on the back porch, leather from jackets makes household accessories (throw pillows, book covers, picture frames), sweaters can be sewn into patchwork throws.
- *Make a paradigm shift in your mind.* After all, splurging while shopping, like splurging while eating, is all in the mind. If you enjoy shopping in nice stores or even discount stores but have no budget for regular escapades out and about, you don't have to go cold turkey. I know of people who go to the mall, buy a few great things, then return them the following week. But I say why waste time in the customer service line? I enjoy haunting favorite shops like Pier One or even Ross, imagining I have a certain amount of money to spend. I pick out only things I love and put them in my basket, imagining where I'll place them and how I'll use them. At the end of an hour, I've had a great time! Then I go around and put them all back. Sound weird? Maybe, but it works in satisfying that shopping drive. It's a great feeling to

go home, having had all the fun of a shopping goddess, but spending absolutely nothing. The next day I almost always realize I really didn't need any of those things. If I can't stop thinking about one item or another, I go back and buy it. (A week later I usually realize I didn't need that either!)

PART 2

My Life
AS A ROOM

EIGHT

Hot Pot
HAVEN

I perfectly remembered ... the crummy linoleum on my aunt's kitchen floor, graying beige speckled with black, and how it wore away to all black near the sink, and how at its most worn places, rotten wood showed through. And how all those cousins ... stood at the sink with us older kids, in a ring around my aunt. And how close I felt to them all, how much a part of the wheel.

Anne Lamott

Two plump, dark-haired women sit in the sun-splashed earth outside a large kitchen near Petah Tikva, a suburb of Tel Aviv. They are the kitchen help on a peanut farm. Most of the morning they pick tiny black stones out of huge cotton sacks of rice, the dietary staple. The women have done this for years, chattering away in Arabic, laughing, sharing gossip in the orange-fragrant air.

When I arrive to work alongside them, it is from a fast-paced kitchen position at an Austrian B&B. Our specialties there were cordon bleu and linser torte. A lover of Mediterranean food, I was hoping to learn to make shish kebab and baklava in the Middle East. Instead, I'm invited to sit alongside a low bench in the sunshine. I join these women in the culling of rice. Their language is beautiful, the sounds quick and bright. But although the sun is gloriously warm in January, coming halfway around the globe to pick stones out of rice disgruntles me.

In Austria I'd been hired to clean bedrooms. One drizzly afternoon, after the linens were washed, ironed, and put back on the beds, I went to the kitchen. Within an hour I'd stirred together a batch of cookies from scratch. When the chocolate-drop darlings were released from the oven, B&B staff gravitated to the kitchen from all corners of the house. Within weeks I was no longer making beds but was baking cakes, pies, and cinnamon rolls. Later I made breakfasts, lunches, and three-course dinners.

Having traveled from a gourmet kitchen in Austria to a primitive Arabic kitchen, I had no way of knowing that the most important culinary lessons had not yet begun.

January passed under Israeli skies. The buzz of military planes was as consistent as the sunshine. I realized there was no reason to accelerate the time it takes to go through a sack of rice looking for tiny stones. I learned to sit for long hours without my primal Western agitation. *Hurry* is not a word Middle-Eastern people understand. *Punctual* is an unheard-of concept. Preparation for a dinner of wild rabbit or lamb, greens, and (you guessed it!) rice takes the time it takes, that's all. What I learned to value as much as the flair of serving a nourishing meal was enjoying the company and the organic process. The twinkle in the dark eyes of the two women passing time on the sunny kitchen steps became, for me, as much inspiration as the food itself. If no other room in a home is sanctuary, certainly the kitchen is.

Since ancient times no more worthy endeavor has existed than to feed others. Abraham and Sarah prepared a special meal for three strangers who eventually revealed themselves as messengers from God. In fact, Scripture says it was the Lord himself who appeared to Abraham.[1] Thousands of years later Jesus repeatedly used food as a metaphor for life. After his resurrection Jesus asked his disciple Peter: "Do you love Me?" When Peter answered in the affirmative, Jesus said, "Feed My sheep,"[2] referring to spiritual nourishment. In Matthew's account Jesus also told his followers that "whoever gives one of these little ones only a cup of cold water . . . shall by no means lose his reward."[3] How much proof do we need that the kitchen itself is a place of worship? Setting a glass of cold milk on the table for a hungry kid is a way to honor God. The work we do in the kitchen is less about elegant style, handy gadgets, and glamorous space than it is about the love and purity of heart that empower the work.

In the kitchen, as in life, "Blessed are the poor in spirit" is more than a quaint phrase originated by an itinerant preacher long ago. I visited Poland long before the collapse of the Iron Curtain and the democratic reforms of Lech Walesa. At that time Poland was a hungry nation full of warmhearted people stunned silent by an iron leash connecting them to communism. Despite harsh conditions, a young mother living refugee style in a mountain cabin served me and the other Americans with whom I was traveling a three-course dinner. Her husband had been fired from his job because he was a practicing Christian. Forced into the mountains to raise their son, the small family lived off their miniscule profit from a newspaper kiosk in an isolated village.

Our Western entourage had come surreptitiously to bring Christian books to Poland. We had smuggled hundreds of them across the border in a van with hidden compartments. But our hosts, Marta and André, were instead an inspirational text for us. Insisting we stay for dinner, rosy-cheeked Marta gathered mushrooms and served up a luscious cream soup. It was followed by sausage and potatoes, then mousse. Only afterward did I learn she had prepared the entire meal on a single hot plate in a room she called her "kitchen." No other appliances were to be seen.

Marta had stood in separate lines for the sausage—a rare "supplement" when meat was available at all, then for the potatoes, and then for the cream. No doubt the cost and her offering a week's worth of food to us was a sacrifice. Yet her graciousness was all we saw.

After the meal, once darkness had fallen, we westerners shuttled our precious literature from the van. We carried it into the cabin as if we were bequeathing a fortune.

Marta expressed her gratitude as we left on that snowy January day. "But if you come again," she said wistfully, "please bring oranges. We haven't had oranges for years."

Marta's request surprised us. Treasure may not look the same to all of us. But it is probably closer to what you'd find in the simplest of kitchens than in any other room—including a library of precious volumes.

I think of Marta whenever I eat oranges and hope that she can now get them by the bagful.

I brought Marta to mind when starting my own writing business out of my home and struggling to put food on the table. During this difficult period a telephone interview with a Christian personality turned out to be a challenge, but not because she was in any way ungracious. It was my own interior stuff with which I was at war. Denalyn Lucado, wife of author Max Lucado and a former missionary to Rio de Janeiro, had a lot to tell me—stories of life with children and what makes a house a home. The previous week her family had moved into what she called a French country farm-style home in Texas. There I was, a journalist listening to a tale of transition from a tough missionary existence to the good life in the United States, and *I* was the one who had the problem.

Newly divorced and struggling to hang on to my small ram-shackle home, I thought Denalyn's former life as a missionary sounded idyllic compared to the struggle of raising three children on my own. I was trying to keep my sanity with a deadline to meet by eight o'clock the next morning and a dinner of fish sticks in the oven. I have to admit that while cooking dinner in my galley-style kitchen that evening, I felt a twinge—well, let's call it a *surge*—of jealousy. I got cynical.

Isn't it easy, I internalized, *to create pleasant memories with your children when you have a faithful husband who is a wonderful father and whose fabulous spiritual gifts purchased a home with a French country kitchen, including a fireplace, no less?*

Lucado is a gracious and humble woman, thus it was completely apparent that my envious feelings arose from my own stuff. But I kept struggling with them. I brought to mind the radiant smile of Marta living in exile, producing a feast on one small hot plate. I brought to mind the twinkling eyes of the two Arab women living peacefully in a country rife with racial hostilities. I remembered the faces of Haitian mothers I had known who considered themselves fortunate to offer a banana or piece of sugarcane to their children for dinner.

Since speaking with Lucado, I've come full circle, and honestly, I bless her gorgeous kitchen—although it took a while for me to do so! Mine may not be French, but it's definitely country. Okay, my kitchen is missing Euro ambience, but it makes up for that in simple abundance (emphasis on *simple*). When I put on the music of Claude Debussy and serve French onion soup in bread bowls, you'd hardly miss the Provence tablecloth or the crackling fire.

Some of the world's best movies take place primarily, and most inspirationally, in the cookery. *Babette's Feast* is a Danish film about an artistic French woman who serves up sensational gourmet fare for a group of pietistic Scandinavians. In their rigid desire to avoid carnal desires, they make a pact to refuse admitting they enjoy the food. The result is a winsome surprise. *Like Water for Chocolate* is a sexy Mexican film tying rituals associated with cooking to our sensuality. *Tortilla Soup* tells the story of an American/Hispanic Los Angeles family whose lives revolve around the loving preparation and beautiful presentation of Sunday meals by their father. And who would miss *Chocolat* with Juliette Binoche and the delectable Johnny Depp? The film made sharing café au lait and chocolate truffles with the man you love absolutely mandatory.

These themes move us because our earliest and most important—positive or negative—childhood experiences begin in the kitchen. One's most vivid memories, say experts, are induced by the olfactory glands. The image of kitchen taps emotion because our senses of taste and scent are associated with the most elemental of human needs—the necessity not just of eating but of dining. No matter where you travel around the globe or how things change, the human need for food and fellowship does not.

The ultimate kitchen, boasts *Time* magazine, is equipped with stainless-steel appliances, a kitchen island, a full wine rack, and easy-to-care-for granite countertops. I have none of these things, but a one-hundred-year-old copper soup pot hangs above my kitchen sink reminding me of lessons I've learned from the kitchens of my life:

Sweet things are best when made from scratch.
The hearty stews in which we find ourselves leave us
strengthened.
Fragile soufflés are mastered with practice.

The bread of life is most nourishing when kneaded into stories.

Picking black stones from the rice of my experience is a thankless task, but it is an essential ingredient to every single day.

soul PROJECT

Make a Small Space Sacred

Classic craftsmanship and experienced building set one house or home apart from another. You don't need a large space to raise a large family. If your goal is togetherness, splurge on activities rather than square feet. Engage repeatedly in endeavors that stimulate an emotional tug. Use the four big principles of experienced decorators to make small things seem larger.

- *Eliminate visual obstacles and dead ends.* Exaggerate praise for little tasks. You'll up the enthusiasm quotient every day when you start noticing and acknowledging what kids do right.
- *Choose a light color palette.* Being positive and energetic will make the people around you feel more capable of contributing. *Voila!* You'll have a bright happy family.
- *Create illusions of openness.* A ski weekend or trip to a theme park are not the ultimate holidays. You can create awe and laughter in your own backyard through a family carnival, kids' treasure hunt, or neighborhood pet parade.
- *Draw the eye upward.* Plan a worship service at a lake or along a river. Build an altar of rocks. Climb to a high place at sunrise and serve a simple meal. The canopy of family is as big as the sky and as large as your faith.

NINE

Table
D'HÔTE

We all need something to believe in, something good, beautiful, or true. If only we could find a concept so inspiring that we'd march headlong into life, convinced of our purpose and radiating belief, our story meant for stained glass.

Kelee Katillac

As a four-year-old taken to church each Sunday, I begged my mother to sit in the balcony so we could be close to the stained-glass windows. High above the pulpit, distanced from the fiery Baptist preacher, I felt safe, surrounded by light filtered through color.

Years later, while studying the cathedrals of Europe in a college class, I was mesmerized by the architecture. As sanctuaries for lofty ideas and corporate worship, these structures fed the spirit and soul of humankind.

Somewhere between the First Baptist Church of Pratt, Kansas, and that first visit to Notre Dame Cathedral in Paris two decades later, I found what interior designer and author Kelee Katillac writes about: a belief that my own life is no less a stained-glass story—light filtered through color.[1]

Where else in a house are these things more evident than in our dining areas? Over a meal—whether at the backyard picnic table or a living room coffee table—the act of breaking bread together is a formal "yes" to spiritual significance. Wherever we share a meal, we possess an inherent need to go beyond simple nourishment of our bodies and to eat mindfully in the presence of others.

Like stained-glass depictions in churches, we are reminded in the dining room of our need not simply to eat but to eat together. Remember Jesus feeding five thousand strangers with a few fish and loaves of bread? Or Jesus turning water into wine for a wedding party? Or Jesus sharing his last supper with his closest friends? Incorporating the sacred into our sustenance, the place we eat is table d'hôte—a place of communion.

The hard-packed dirt floor of a mud house, swept meticulously clean, is the most poignant dining table at which I've eaten. Upon arriving at a refugee camp in Gaza, still Israeli territory in the 1970s, boys appeared and began flinging small stones at me and my American friend. Our Palestinian hostess shooed away the boys and welcomed us with a huge smile into her earthen home. Sitting cross-legged on cotton rugs, we took food with our fingers from a platter of spicy chicken and rice that had been placed on the floor between us. There were no plates, utensils, or napkins; no tablecloth, place mats, or centerpiece. Who needed those? Our friend's hospitality was both décor and service. Her meal was a time-honored observance of what we held in common despite political, religious, or racial differences: our humanity, our faith, our respect.

Summers in Europe influenced me too. My favorite dining room is the great outdoors. A grassy-knoll fanatic, I recently learned that the late queen mother of England was also a picnic epicure, which is after all a Victorian art. Paintings of the era depict ladies in white dresses and large hats spreading wonderful food on delicate tablecloths. My picnics happen from a backpack. They are spread on a sensible blanket along a river or served from a sunny rock. I like to hype special occasions with a picnic or a three-course breakfast under my backyard aspen tree. Afternoon tea may be served on a table bedecked in pansies. For barbeques I set my red, white, and blue dishes alongside potted geraniums in cobalt planters.

Europe's dining rooms are more elaborate than America's where design experts insist the formal dining room is dead. It no longer fits our on-the-go lifestyle, they say. That may be true. Even in my dining room proper, things are not necessarily elegant or traditional. I have set up a home office in one corner of my dining room because I like working in the heart of my home. Here you'll find everything from a fax machine to my mother's flowered teacups. Stainless-steel desk accessories are shadowed by tall indoor palms rising out of corners. Hung on opposite walls are a painting of red shoes (a personal metaphor for me, as for Dorothy of Oz, of a woman's energy in the world) and a print of Marc Chagall's Jerusalem skyline. My beat-up computer takes center stage on the desk, while just a few feet away a cloisonné Italian chandelier hangs above the table. Here, my "devotee of femininity and tradition" self coexists with my "gypsy and lover of whimsy" self.

Still, the dining table, although no longer associated with propriety and primness, is the place where we sit up straight. In this room as in no other, we make intentional connection on a regular basis. It is where we look each other in the eye because we are centered around a common essential activity. If you believe that every time someone looks you in the eye, he or she is asking, "Do you love me?" you may find the answer to this unspoken question at the dinner table.

After all, a meal is a respite from the cares of the day, the wounds of enemies, the playground of our lives, the grueling work that is our livelihood. Whether it's breakfast in a nook or a grand buffet dinner, the atmosphere in which we eat is layered with nuances of spirituality—the storms weathered, the waves ridden.

The Jewish ritual of the Shabbat, or Sabbath, meal on Friday evening at sundown is the quintessential dining experience. Candles are lit before daylight disappears from the sky. The blessing is sung. Bread is broken. Wine, signifying abundance, is poured. Participating in this ceremonial meal is a privilege I was graced to experience during my stay in Israel. I took from it the lingering emotional impact of tradition and respect for family and national heritage.

In Switzerland, the land of Reformed Christian tradition, I awoke to the tinkle of cowbells from a nearby mountainside and the smell of coffee on my first-ever day in Europe. The four weeks I lived and worked at L'Abri Fellowship community in Huemoz have become a predominant motif in my stained-glass story.

There, in 1970, Edith Schaeffer was matron and hostess, opening her chalet home to young people from around the world, hundreds every year. The long narrow table wedged into a small dining area was punctuated with flickering light. Guests spoke late into the evening with Francis Schaeffer, theologian and philosopher who attracted a worldwide audience. Food was served with artful simplicity, appealing to the eye as well as the palate. Candlelight and conversation were as necessary to dining as the bread basket or water glasses.

Ever since my travels abroad, Christian, Jewish, and Islamic traditions of hospitality have been a part of every meal in my home. I can just as easily begin a meal with a silent moment as with a memorized grace sung at the table or a spontaneously composed prayer of thanksgiving. The form of prayer isn't important. The act of reverence before a meal can be communicated in a variety of original ways, yet we offer praise to the same everlasting Father. In the act of blessing a meal, we honor what we are there for: getting closer to each other and to God.

Several years ago, I took my two younger daughters to a beachfront bed-and-breakfast. Leyah was leaving for college within days and didn't want to go; I insisted—for my sake. We walked on a rain-soaked beach and spent the evening reading by a little fire while listening to the surf break just yards away. Next morning, breakfast was served at tables set for six. What happened at ours is one of those things that can't be planned or purchased. Leyah, Lissa, and I ended up at a table with a photojournalist and his wife, a writer, from the East Coast. Their friend, the owner of the B&B, a stunning dynamo of a woman, joined us at the table.

I wondered if the girls and I were going to feel isolated from the conversation. Instead, we were drawn into it. Our fellow diners were as fascinated with our family's trio as we were by their bright philosophical ideas and tales of travels afar. An animated, profound dialogue took place, in which my daughters were included and engaged. It was a turnabout to the experience of Abraham and Sarah, who entertained strangers at Mamre. Here we were at an Oregon beach B&B, where strangers entertained us—a stained-glass story if ever there was one. You never know

85

when table d'hôte will happen, angels and all, but the possibilities exist wherever bread is broken.

When my two-year-old granddaughter eats lasagna, she carefully separates the tiny broccoli florets and strips of red pepper from pieces of pasta. Tomato sauce covers both hands, squishes between outstretched fingers, and smears across her cheeks. Tendrils of her curly hair become caked with bits of vegetables and cheese.

In this scene I see the Eucharist.

Dining is art.

I see light filtered through color as the essence of our lives, never more than around our dining tables.

When we serve meals, we are creating stories meant for stained glass. What will yours communicate?

*soul*PROJECT

Create Your Own Rituals

Smart. Understated. Forgiving. These are words some designers use to describe interiors that maximize livability. How can you create rituals at home that invite you and your family to rejuvenate a holy sense of place? Here are some experts' ideas to build on.

- *Seek serendipity.* Welcome unexpected experiences as Sarah welcomed strangers to her home.
- *Attend to details that amplify ambience.* Spend time setting the scene to get people in the mood.
- *Play down unnecessary drama.* Ignore unwelcome intruders such as grumpy moods or overindulgent expectations.

- *Define the cathedral quotient.* What helps your family members feel loved by the others? Brainstorm ways to make those connections.
- *Get the most bang from your "construction" buck.* Invest in rituals that improve with age. Go for what's interesting over what's traditional or trendy. Find out what your kids love and do it!
- *Create a lavish focal point for limited time together.* Play it up with things you know will generate pleasure in the experience: games, food, physical interaction, ambience.

TEN

Great Room,
GOOD LIVING

My gift to myself has been to make my home a sanctuary—a place that rises up to meet me every time I enter the front door. . . . Home isn't just a residence you purchase or a place you retreat to at the end of a day—it's the sense of yourself that you carry with you no matter where you lay your head.

Oprah Winfrey

The other day I heard a design and construction executive claim that today's families are looking for homes that balance comfort with multitasking. This, he observed, is changing what a house looks like inside. Walls are coming down in order to allow for more family togetherness and personal space in the same area of the home.

Architects can call the invention of the "great room" a twenty-first-century concept, but what's so twenty-first century about it? How many of us have been living this way for decades?

My family and I lived in five different houses on two continents before settling, and every house had great rooms. In the place we would ultimately call home, the living room blended into the kitchen, which blended into the home office, which blended into the backyard. The living room quickly became the great room when we moved in, because the cozy pull of heat from a woodstove kept us centered. In our modest house, "personal space" simply meant that bit of cushion underneath you and whatever sofa throw was available at the moment. So while the room accommodated everything we wanted or needed to do, we were often rubbing shoulders with somebody else—whether we wanted to or not. But wearing off rough edges is what family is all about.

The word *comfort* means different things to different people. In our family it meant sitting side by side with our feet tangled up on the coffee table, arguing about who said what, while multitasking the evening away. If by "comfort," designers mean the magnitude of a home, what could be more irrelevant? Every family represents a different configuration of space, time, tradition, and place.

When I picked up *The Not So Big House* by Sarah Susanka, I was amazed at how huge—in number of square feet—the "not so big" houses in her book actually were. You may live in a home the size of a lodge, in a studio apartment, or in a dormitory room. But no matter where you live, your great room is about who you are with the people who live there too. A great room is not about architecture; it is about where you invest your presence.

Comfort means, if nothing else, a safe place to fall. Curl up on a pillow by the fire or in your battered recliner. Take off your shoes. Push clutter aside and replace it with a plate of your favorite munchies. Even when life goes on the skids, comfort is what happens when families go through it together. A great room is where you sit and rock, mending torn seams or a broken heart. Sometimes you spill out your feelings and the words fall wrong. In a worst-case scenario, like the evening my children's father told them he was moving out, comfort means shoring up the damage. The great room acts as a container for that most sacred family treasure: pain.

Ultimately, the great-living room is about life—exactly the way it is at any given moment. As such, it's the room in which the furniture—and the family emotional matrix—is most often rearranged.

Why not? Isn't life meant for grand experiment, not to be hoarded or allowed to grow stagnant? Live it right out loud. Give it your attention. Give it away. Life is a great big canvas; throw all the color on it you can. Wisdom is knowing when to let go of things and when to hang on tightly to what really counts.

I always loved something Helen Thames Raley, the first lady of a Texas university, used to say: "A woman's job is to make life better, to make tomorrow better than today." There's plenty of opportunity to exercise that message in my home. I've learned to thrive in change, even changes I did not want. Spills and scrapes and messes—what better ways to transform a mansion or a cottage into a place for simply great living?

With kids around, my living room never stayed tidy or clean. Their shoes and books and sweaters lay everywhere. Bickering filled the crevices between walls and rafters. But there was also dancing on these floors. It was here that we hauled out Christmas decorations and pulled in the tree year after year, heaping it with baubles and lights. This is where rounds of Pictionary and Cranium kept us knitted together in laughter and tests of cleverness. Here is where we piled high on the floor the sofa pillows and dozens of videos in search of just the thing for a night at home. The kaleidoscopic colors of firelight have reflected off these walls. It was in our great living room that we worked out life's issues, adapting, integrating, and rearranging our lives to fit new realities.

And it is here that I am still doing that. Just as I celebrate the fact that days of raising high-maintenance girls are behind me, I turn around and find my granddaughter a toddler with her chubby hands all over everything. A daughter calls to say she's bringing home a boyfriend from college, and I realize that painting the dining room ceiling can't be put off another day. I wake up with a backache and know my beloved but battered desk chair has got to go. Paint stains on the carpet bring to mind Leyah's early oil paint experiments—where else but in the middle of the living room floor? Today those spots of color are testament to beautifully composed portraits and a budding career. A New Year's Eve party (in my absence) ended with a living room cake fight. That just means more laughter when we spot bits of dried icing still stuck to the ceiling.

None of us will forget that middle-of-the-night escapade when junior high boys TPed our house. One of them left a poop pie (his own!) right on the doorstep as a practical joke. The girls and I unknowingly tiptoed through it in the dark, then tracked it back through the living room. (Yes, this really happened.) But I still have the contrite and courteous note the joker wrote on a beautiful scented card. His mother brought him over to scrub my entire carpet on his hands and knees. Now, whenever we pass in the grocery store, we share a secret smile, and I can't help but laugh.

What is it about your living room that makes it "great"? What brings you comfort? How do you use your personal space and re-create your persona in the details of a room? How does your home fit the way you live? If you called a stylist to solve a decorating problem, she would work with the material that's there. Throwing out the bad stuff and accentuating the good, she is there to create solutions that work for everybody. Be the stylist of your own great room, your life, your journey, your family feel-good climate. You never have to start from scratch. Sometimes you just need to fine-tune and finish what you started. At other times you need to update, turning hectic to haven.

A Carl Larsson-esque (remember the Swedish master of home-life paintings?) appeal surfaced when I realized that beauty starts from the inside out. My previously rustic-cabin style was transformed when I painted all the inside natural wood trim white, along with whatever pieces of furniture were not antique pine. Bright and airy, the visual difference created a change in mood I didn't expect. The furniture suddenly came into its own. And more: Now I ask questions that make me conscious of thinking about myself and my world in new ways too.

A woman's spirituality is intimately interwoven with her sense of place. Experience and emotion are indissolubly linked in memory with home. In fact, a house symbolizes all the states of mind through which we pass.

Paul Tournier wrote, "At every moment of our lives an ineffaceable network of correlations is being set up between our inner world and the external world. One will always recall the other."[1]

On a national level, it appears that we are engaged in a passionate, nostalgic search at home for something that has been lost within ourselves. I suppose, as long as we're human, the place where we live ekes eternity out of us.

How transformational can a place become when you connect with your own spirit there, setting the stage for a network between your inner world and the external?

I do this when I practice what I call "puttering." A kind of serenity comes over me when I move around my house studying the objects of my affection and looking for ways to create different harmonious groupings. Sometimes I move a chair closer to a window or a stack of books nearer to the woodstove. In any case, when I move about, touching objects and repositioning them, I am oddly soothed. Surely this isn't mysterious. Perhaps this is, pure and simple, the laying on of hands the apostle Paul spoke about. We hold objects of history, legacy, affection, and beauty, and in doing so we find pleasure and create art. Nothing is ever perfect or final, and that is in fact the charm of interacting with our homes in a spiritual way.

Showplace glam? No. The carpet in my house shows stains from years of wear, and the refrigerator sends a shudder and grunt to the living room every forty minutes. But in all of this, a great room is being created every day. My place on Ladigo Street offers a place to put up your feet or get up on them and dance.

*soul*PROJECT

Leave Your Heart at Home

I printed big round numbers and letters: 616 SOUTH OAK. The forms fit perfectly between the wide lines in my Red Chief tablet. The address applied to a small white house on a red brick street in a small town of white houses, Pratt, Kansas. A nondescript town, it lies at the geographical center point of America. My name was like the land: *Smith.* The name was so devoid of any kind of mystique that that fact itself became its charm.

In the heartland there are no destination resorts. It is the kind of place you drive across to get somewhere else. Bare and dusty, the plains are vulnerable to nature's whims: wind, drought, pelting rain, tornadoes. Immortalized in *The Wizard of Oz* by its contrast to the colorful land of munchkins and yellow brick roads, Dorothy's understatement about Oz has become a classic: "Toto, I don't think we're in Kansas anymore."

It was in Kansas that my grandparents survived the Great Depression and the Dust Bowl days. They lost three farms but hung on to the fourth in the face of incredible odds. Clinging tenaciously to the land, they raised four sons. Plain folks, they worked the soil, persevering in that flat windswept place. I always wondered, *What made them stick it out?*

My grandparents are now buried in the earth of this heartland. And over time, I've begun to understand why they stuck it out. As far as I know, they had no dreams of being anywhere else. They didn't give up when the going got tough. They didn't go shopping for a better place when the wheat crop withered in the field. They discovered that when you lie close to the heart of someone or someplace for a long time, you hear and see what others don't. The secrets taught by holding on and hanging in there turn out to be exactly what you are looking for.

Reflect on this and write a letter to the place in your home where you've lived some of your greatest moments and weathered a threatening storm. What does that place say to you now? What do you want to tell this place about coming through the gales and forces of life itself? Put your letter in a spot for treasures in your home as a secret missive to someone in a future generation or someone who may inhabit this same space, a person you may never meet.

ELEVEN

Boudoir
SWEET

If home is about sanctuary and shelter, then the bedroom is its ultimate expression, the very heart of the matter.

Victoria magazine

My favorite weekend getaway on the Oregon coast, the Sylvia Beach Hotel, is laced through and through with sense of place and boudoir sweet. For an avid reader, this literary hotel (complete with the Tables of Content dining room) doubles as a spa for the soul. Every room is named after an author and decorated in the theme of his or her work. You can spend your stay in the ambient femininity of the Emily Dickinson Room, in the virile humor of the Mark Twain Room, in the fun-studded primary colors of the Doctor Seuss Room (goldfish in a bowl, bedside), or in the "rose is a rose" elegance of the Gertrude Stein Room.

It is to this creative establishment that I've come alone when fighting the blues or when wanting to renew my sense of the poetic against practical demands. After becoming single again, I received inspiration from the Sylvia Beach Hotel to reinvent my bedroom. The irony is that in its first "life," my bedroom was the garage of our small house. This fact makes me marvel because the allegory seems too perfect: a boudoir (a word from the French that means "to pout") that was once a garage and then a bedroom for a marriage that was not what it seemed. Reincarnating the room a third time into a single-again honeymoon haven is proof that any place so poisoned can, indeed, become sweet again. For romance has little to do with a man.

My personal renaissance brought about such renovation with panache. I took something ugly and made from it something beautiful.

Guess what? I learned along the way. I get to do that with my life as the interior designer of my own experience on this earth.

The bedroom comes closer than any other room in defining the multifaceted soul of my life story's lead character. After all, a bedroom facilitates the unconscious. It is where the last visual image each night and the first visual image each morning feed my psyche and spirit. It is the place I dream, the place I watch myself in the mirror—wash, dress, and pamper this incredible body that at times has been abused with too little sleep, poor food choices, and lack of exercise yet has still kept me moving and breathing for more than half a century. The bedroom, more than any other, influences my dreams, thoughts, self-talk, imagination, and inspiration to live my passions.

Shortly before I revamped my bedroom, I was asked to model in a local fashion show and surprised myself by being quickly affirmative. Then again, who wouldn't say yes when offered a free haircut and color, facial, and style analysis? The experience taught me lessons I needed. When I showed up at the boutique to pick out clothes for the fashion show, my excitement immediately dissipated. The store manager had already selected what she wanted me to model. I sought out the fashion coordinator and whispered in horror, "I would never actually wear these outfits in public!"

"Oh no," she answered when she saw them. "These are *not* you." She proceeded to weave through the shop choosing clothes for me while I browsed in one corner. Eventually she showed up, arms laden with chic capris and peasant tops, simple dresses with classic lines, turquoise beads, and bangles.

"How could you know exactly what I'd wear?" I asked, delighted.

"Because I'm trained to recognize personal style," she offered, calling mine part town-and-country and part ethnic-artsy.

Bingo.

How she nailed that when she barely knew me, I'm still not sure. I do know, regardless of my experiments over the years with whatever's trendy, that I've always come back again and again to simple lines and bold, solid colors, anything beaded, and clothing that moves or is cut at angles. Frilly cuts and flowery patterns don't work for me, and they won't work for my bedroom either. So I make changes to my boudoir décor within my signature style, expressed differently as I move through transitions of age, calling, and location. When I was married, raising children, and working as a magazine and book editor, I didn't even have time to dream about signature style, let alone give it conscious attention, and least of all pay for it. But life is short. The tables have turned, and I'm here to tell about it.

Starting out all over again was like being let loose in a wildflower field, complete with fragrance, color, and newly felt freedom to wander and wonder. My boudoir self deserved some complementary attention. A little paint. A lot more love. Thoughtful redefinition. *Why not start with that archetype of intimacy, sexuality, and personal mystique,* I wondered, *the bed?* It's been said that men prefer four-post beds, preferably spiraling (*ooh-la-la*), and that women look for sleigh beds or curved head- and footboards—resembling the womb shape.

I didn't want a conventional headboard at all. I got a new bed (a donation from my darling mother) and moved it under the front window, which was exactly the same width. I layered sheer embroidered curtains, French fabricated and picked up at a closeout sale, for privacy and as an artful crown over white pillow shams and duvet. A swoop of gauzy fabric, twisted and hung a little funkily from the ceiling, created just the off-center romantic look I hoped for. It was a frolicsome solution, and no pennies or time were spent shopping for a mass-produced piece of furniture that actually serves little purpose.

A woman's bed should be easy to make and should mesh with her personal style. Sophisticated? Glamorous? Bohemian? Urban glitz? Every woman's expression of sensuality will be different. Do you prefer to snuggle into goose down or wrap up in superthin blankets? Do you like oversized pillows or standard pillows? White on crème bedding or jewel-toned velvets? Netted bed-drapes with silky fringed tassels or curtains drawn around a canopy structure? The details you choose should inspire you (and your spouse!) to hang out in your intimate cloister.

My own interpretation of "sensuous" leads me to seek the unexpected. Bias-cut white satin gowns (thrift-store finds) drape across a window on white satin hangers. The walls elicit a kicky *espièglerie*: a showplace for original objects where flaws and stray brushstrokes say, "Someone touched this." The bohemian in me was vitalized when I "ragged on" a flesh-toned terra-cotta paint and coated that with flourishes of textured pearl glaze. Candlelight—and I—look great against the appeal of the Old World ambience. In such a boudoir, I become my own muse.

A bedroom is your place of retreat within the refuge you call home. Its rituals are encouraged by the details with which you surround yourself: A crystal goblet of water refilled every evening at bedtime? A pretty trivet waiting for your morning latte, sipped while you prop yourself against mounds of pillows? Cuddling at dawn with the best of company—favorite books camped beside your bed? In the evening is journaling inspired by the imagined history of a hand-pieced quilt? My quilt is nubby with tiny loops of thread, the blocks worn to near translucence. Like the woman who created it from scraps of her life, I write my story in a blank volume—one stitch at a time. How about wallpaper of your own invention? I created a wall covered with *Victoria* and *Country Living* magazine photographs: a collage of golden pinks and pale reds around the window at the head of my bed. An altar reminds me to pause and remember, thanking God for the people and things I love. Photographs or outdoorsy things perch on my bedroom shelf as icons: seashells, river pebbles, a bouquet of dried roses, pieces of driftwood lashed with leather and tied with feathers. These are personal ways to thank God and remind myself of his love.

A bedroom is the most intimate room in your home. Soft lights and soothing or stirring music invite disclosure of secrets. For married couples, it is the place to explore the landscape of the person you love in murmured conversation or tactile pleasure. Let both moonlight and thunder ripple through the windows. Get enveloped in the scent of body oil and the sound of giggles mixed with sighs. Let the space be filled with things that vivify knowing. Because *frumpy* isn't even a word in the boudoir, you must romance yourself long before you romance someone else. Live, the Turkish mystic Rumi said, "until life itself becomes the lover." Any woman must know how to create amour for herself.

Isn't the spirit of in-love-ness, along with its excitement, desire, and passionate exchange, exactly the dynamic you want your bedroom to incite?

In the celebratory mode of boudoir sweet, I'm sure I've broken a hundred rules of haute décor, but the result is inspired by the drama of life itself.

The bedroom I would die for is the khaki safari tent that served as part-time boudoir of Karen Blixen, aka Isak Dinesen, whose life was portrayed by Meryl Streep in *Out of Africa*. Dinesen was a woman after my own heart, for she chose adventure over comfort, and she even knew the most luxurious hotels couldn't hold a candle to the place that holds your heart.

*soul*PROJECT

Change the Bed— and Your Frame of Mind

Puk, puk, puk padooooo! "Every chick's coop has gotta have a little cock-a-doodle-do," insist interior decorators and *Home Swell Home* authors Cynthia Rowley and Ilene Rosenzweig. The bedroom is the place to get sexy and sassy. Of any room in the house, this one has got to be *le chambre de bebe*. The "babe's" room is about whatever makes you feel juicy. Keep the intimacy quotient, and your outlook on life, forever fresh with these ideas:

- *Make room for the luxury of chairs*, which can add emotional content to a room. Chairs represent personal presence because they imply a welcome to sit down and be present with yourself. You can throw your clothes across a chair's arms, curl up in a chair's seat for a cozy phone call, and feast your eyes upon a chair's pretty face first thing each morning.

- *Go for the sensual.* Subtle scents create allure. Mellow lighting and mood lamps—no overhead bulbs—provide the cuddly feeling you yearn for. An open window with its wafts of fresh air is the best partner for a good night's sleep.

- *Increase your sashay factor by brightening your boudoir.* Whether your style is floral inspired or the classic clean lines of a prairie at daybreak, surprise yourself with detailed accessories in a contrasting style. Ground feminine fabric with masculine touches of black or dark blue in throw rugs, wall hangings, or small pillows.

- *Make music and inspiration-only reading essential at bedtime.* But no radios, please. Get a CD player with a remote so you can skip jarring songs and let a favorite artist lull you into a positive frame of mind. Switch the CD to automatic shutoff as you burrow down. Give yourself an upper by reading aloud from an awesome piece of classic literature as music and lights fade.

- *Lavish yourself in a luscious, creamy, moisturizing body lotion before you hit the sack.*

- *And don't forget to say your prayers.*

TWELVE

Where Lullabies
LINGER

Childhood is the morning time of life when all is change and wonder.... Childhood is for exploring ... for running and reaching and
touching and seeing and tasting and hearing and learning.

Joan Walsh Anglund

Celia is five years old, that enchanting age when a little
girl still believes that dreams come true. She experiences
every day that the glass slipper fits. She knows inherently
what the psalmist must remind the adult: that she is *wonderfully*
made. Celia shares a bedroom with a brother who is still a toddler.
But in Celia's mind, her bedroom is her own hobbit paradise. It
is a place of gentle make-believe creatures and a treasure trove
of cast-off costume jewelry and silky clothes. These ignite her
favorite pastime: gypsy princess play. Celia's pleasure in plushy
fabrics and jewel-toned anything surfaces in the way she com-
bines raw materials with imagination. She likes anything with

ribbons, buttons, or baubles. She paints pictures of fairies, and in her reverie, they all have iridescent green wings. Her favorite music is produced by a drum she made from an oatmeal box. It is painted red with black polka dots.

Celia's mother, a lithograph artist who teaches printmaking in the schools, feeds the adventure in this most charming of places, her children's bedroom. She understands the cultural standards that make a girl prim and predictable by age seven, and, later, that make a boy numb his feelings trying to become a man. A child's room, she believes, should be a place where a kid hangs on as long as possible to spontaneity. It is where a kid can engage in random acts of being real. Celia's mom makes certain her children's room contains a revolving variety of books about faraway places and all kinds of characters. Celia's favorite places to adventure, however, are blank notebooks available to write her own scribbled "stories." She writes before she reads, in imitation cursive with big fat loops and curly scrawls. Her younger brother draws crayon squiggle pictures in the margins.

Other ingredients necessary in kids' play? A parent who is part of the entertainment. A parent to wrestle with, to be tickled by, and to dress up in silly clothes or funny hairstyles! Haven't you noticed that kids can almost smell the emotional presence of an adult? A kid's room where parents dare to tread in their own messy glory is the place where lullabies linger on. This is the place to let down your hair and get goofy for a change. Build a blanket fort and serve crumpets with chilled orange tea. Crawl into the closet for a friendly ghost story. Do a spontaneous puppet show behind the chest of drawers. Inspiration is everywhere.

Kids' rooms are not about external space but about a certain place inside a child who senses vividly who she is. A pilot? A gardener? A dancer? A cop? Isn't there a kid inside you and me who understands what celebrating life is all about? The spirit of experimentation is how our gifts emerge and grow. Since when did the kid in us depend on corporate marketing of media heroes? When you and I were children, didn't we create our own superhero themes?

A kid tinkers around with musical instruments, with Mom and Dad's grown-up tools, and with whatever can be taken apart and put back together in alternative ways. A wooly sock becomes a puppet with button eyes. Big appliance boxes are a miner's tunnel or a cowboy's hideout. Swatches of fun fabric are cut, swathed, and tied into place on birthday dolls. Big fat catalogs are the perfect resource for making mosaic pictures out of tiny torn pieces of paper.

Are children's imaginations stifled when their rooms are decorated with marketed themes? Keep their gray matter growing by giving them space to focus on what juices their own creativity. When rooms are filled with raw material, kids have optimum opportunity to become their own heroes.

As a child, I played on my bed for hours, pretending it was a Conestoga wagon plodding West. No toys were needed apart from a knit shawl and a bonnet borrowed from my grandmother. A scene change called for dramatic capture by Indians, after which I went barefoot and wove my hair into braids. All the action was happening inside my head. One of my own little girls outdid me, though. One day, completing a writing assignment on deadline at the typewriter on the dining table, I had piled up toys and dolls for Leyah to play with, then dove into my work. Later I noticed the room had become totally silent. My four-year-old was sitting stock-still in a little chair in the middle of the floor, staring into space.

I panicked, thinking something was terribly wrong. "Leyah, are you all right? Why don't you play?" I said. "Get your dolls and, please, play house or something!"

Leyah looked up at me as if I were crazy. "Mommy, can't you see I *am* playing?" she asked innocently. "I am the princess, and this is my castle."

Leyah's imaginative play cultivated creative ways to deal with reality because there were no boundaries or corporate-imposed toys. Now grown, she is afraid of nothing—poverty, aloneness, foreign travel, crooks, criminals, or cranks. She knows that she has all the resources she will ever need right inside.

If you don't have children but do have a spare room, create a welcoming environment that also evokes imagination for your guests. Know this: Generic guest rooms are out; personality is in, and the decorating world abounds with options! The best part is that you don't have to spend, spend, spend to make your guest room delightful. Use what you have, and put your décor accessories on a revolving style show. My dream for a guest room became reality as my three children moved into their own lives. I realized that the certain-something look and feel of each room is up to me. A guest room doesn't have to be matronly, practical, or fancy; it just needs to be welcoming.

What do you want to say to your guests as they hit the sack? I asked myself.

Guest room décor is about expressing yourself in a context that exceeds your guests' expectations. I want my guests to be blown away with attention and to know that I'm delighted they've arrived. Simplicity is essential, along with a few radical surprises.

You can nix the chocolates on the pillow and come up with a whole new way to say "sweet dreams." A guest's primary needs are a place for belongings and a feeling of belonging in your place. Allow spacious open tabletops. Leave empty hangers in the closet, and why not tag them with pretty quotes on satin ribbons? To display fresh flowers, use wall vases that don't take up room on a bureau and aren't easily tipped over. Mix and match hand-milled soaps, lotions, and towels, the essential comforts of a stay away from home. You may want to throw a plushy robe over a chair and tuck a pair of fleece socks into the pocket. A tray with bottled water, a pretty glass, and fruit and crackers or mixed nuts is always appreciated. Leave an inspirational quote on the pillow in a pretty card.

To increase the feeling of "no place like home," how about decorating for a favorite aunt with a three-dimensional wall hanging? Grandmother's hand-me-down dress against one wall is reminiscent of times when women didn't always wear jeans. I drape a red cut-glass necklace that belonged to Grandma Daisy over a gold-framed mirror as a symbol of her love of elegant things. Photographs of her in elaborate hats and lavish lace collars add the charm of the gilded age I missed.

For a girlfriend, change out of the Victorian style by replacing Grandma's dress with Mom's. I treasure my mother's fifties-era little black dress, so early "Jackie." In this outfit, Mom looked like the princess she never recognized herself to be. I can change the whole context of a guest room by using that dress to achieve black-and-white elegance. Photographs of Parisian scenes, stored from the girls' old rooms, replace the Victorian motif.

When a granddaughter comes to visit, out come the little table and chairs and tiny tea sets. Yellow gingham with pink toile draped over window and bed make the room seem fairy-tale-like too.

Guest rooms are a work in progress. I used to wonder what to do with all the books I'd collected over the years. Now, when a guest arrives, I pull those I imagine my guest will enjoy and stash them around the room for browsing: Cute volumes of stories for grandmothers. Motivational themes for go-getters. Gardening books, beauty and health magazines, and home design catalogs for girlfriends. I tuck these away in a basket on the floor or poise them on a shelf or bedside table. Photograph or coffee-table books especially make a pleasant exit to the day for a tired traveler.

A small table in a corner of the room can become sacred space when you leave a candle with matches to light it alongside a personal note of welcome. Some small icon from your natural habitat makes it an altar where your guest can be reminded that all good things come from God and where thanks can be given. For my home, that might be a pretty pinecone, a vase of tall grasses, or a bouquet of red and black volcanic stones. It doesn't have to be colorful; it just needs to be a token of the holy sense of place where you live.

You'll find other ways to express hospitality by combing the pages of good books and searching for details in the photographs of home and garden magazines. Tour model homes, and take mental notes when you visit the homes of friends.

A wise woman hears one word and understands two, so give yourself time to ponder. Most important, lend your prayers and your fervent attention to the art of making a stranger feel at home. Seize the sparkle. Take back the night. Your guests will love the difference.

soul PROJECT

Use What You Have to Create Livability

You probably already have everything you need to create the look and feel of a house-becoming-home. The rule of thumb in using what you have is this: See everything in a new way. Can the objects stuffed away in your closets be used for a different purpose, in a different place, or with a new disguise? Try on these ideas.

- *Turn an object upside down or on its side.* Try placing anything in an unusual setting and you'll see marked changes. Things you may have grown tired of suddenly become eccentric bookends, candleholders, or conversation pieces. A vase you inherited, turned upside down, is a pedestal for a photo of the great aunt it belonged to. A garden angel, predictable on the front stoop, might be urban kitsch on your armoire. Books can be turned on their sides as bookends.

- *Paint things in various shades of white.* Almost anything metal, wood, or plastic can be updated and freshened with a coat of cream or wash of pearl. Worn furniture or accessories look totally different with a whitewash. Update with a bowl of seashells in summer or a photo of last year's ski trip in winter.

- *Mat, frame, and hang kids' paintings in unexpected places:* on a bathroom wall, beside a grand mirror, beside school photos in the kitchen, inside the hall closet.

- *Go sugar and spice when painting flea market finds.* Mix bright reds with white and sand colors. Think Cajun and crème. Blend anything brass and bronze or copper for an earthy zest against neutral walls or fabrics.

- *Modern family-friendly objects come into their own among inherited pieces* pulled out of storage in the attic or basement. Mix country with urban/techno style to get a trendy eclectic appeal.

THIRTEEN

Soulful,
SENSUAL BATHING

And you shall wash your linen and keep your body white
In a rainfall at morning and dewfall at night.

Robert Louis Stevenson

Powder your nose? Freshen up? Visit the *rest*room? *Draw* your bubble bath? *Take* a shower? Isn't this chamber we call the bathroom, necessary room, comfort station, or water closet brimming with odd and eccentric images? It is the place of our most intimate daily or hourly rituals. Its symbolism embraces both our primal and civilized instincts. It is a place that may both enhance our personal sensuality and remind us that we cannot escape our physicality.

For the woman always seeking the aesthetic, the bathroom is a good clean challenge. It is the place where a girl looks herself in the eye first thing each morning and last thing at night, encompassing all that may mean. Here she may cast a critical glance at her body or lavish it with personal indulgences: soft plushy towels and hands-on caresses with scented oils, soaps, and lotions. For no other room is there more specialized, intriguing, and inviting ways to create the daily "spa–aah!" effect.

The spa–aah! effect is much more than rituals for hygienic feeling good or looking good. It's an emotional and spiritual makeover too. The body and mind are things, after all, that every woman updates daily. She may begin with her morning bathing routine, but the spa–aah! effect expands as she moves through the different rooms in her house. The effect goes on to encompass the way a woman lives in the wide, wide world; it includes the visual impact she brings to other people, her sensuality, emotional bearing, and spiritual influence.

The spa–aah! effect is mystique from the inside out. A woman uses her mystique, her sense of personality and femininity, to touch and bless the people in her life. Creating the spa–aah! effect is to follow the wisdom of Christian Dior by remembering that zest is the secret of all beauty.

The bathroom is the most enigmatic of rooms, riddled with ancient and contemporary ritual. It is connected with cultural superstitions as well. According to the Celts, for whom water represented a reunion with the womb, a few silver coins in the bath ensured good luck. Adding the first snow of winter to the bath brought good health. Sage wisdom has it that roses in the bath bring love; lavender, happiness; rosemary, creativity; peppermint, revivification; and eucalyptus, freedom from pain. A recipe for romance calls for oranges and fresh mint leaves added to the bath and rubbed on the body—then allowed to air-dry. Do you want beauty? Would you be willing to go to the extremes Cleopatra did? She is said to have bathed regularly in asses' milk.

Bathing involves a religious significance in many cultures. For Muslims and Jews it is associated with purification and holiness. The complex bathing rituals of the Japanese are meant to facilitate mental clarity. Instead of seeing bathing as just a way to get clean like we do in the West, Eastern cultures get clean in separate quarters so that they can bathe. For Native Americans sweat lodges are used to facilitate healing of illness (everything from influenza to pleurisy) as well as to revitalize racial identity. In Finland the sauna is a national institution. It is said that prior to the 1990s there were more saunas than cars in that country.

In Russia the *bania*, or sauna, once included intimate family rituals. A bride, on the day before her wedding, was taken for a sweat bath. Her sweat was collected by pouring milk over her body and catching it in a bowl. The milk was mixed with flour to make a dough. The dough was plastered all over her while she completed her bath, then scraped off and kneaded to make bread for the marriage feast. Childbirth often took place in the *bania* as well. Following a funeral, families gathered not in the dining room for a meal together but in the *bania* to grieve.

In Scandinavia communal bathing in a sauna involves nudity that is as neighborly as a potluck supper. As an American living on a tiny out-of-the-way island in Denmark, the thought of bathing with the postman who lived down the street wasn't exactly my cup of tea. But when the opportunity arose, I jumped right in with my friends just for the experience. Now that I live in Oregon, a hike to one of the many natural hot springs along the Cascade mountain range can mean bathing nude without company.

My favorite bath of all time was around a large vat of muddy black clay at the Dead Sea. The salts and minerals in the clay bring a tingling sensation. I had plastered it on thick and relaxed in the sun—a multitude of chairs are available—allowing it to dry completely. The point is to take time rinsing off in one of the many outdoor showers because the sticky mud adheres between teeth, in hair, and under armpits. Trying to get it all off brings laughter to last a lifetime.

Back in downtown Jerusalem, I visited the Turkish baths more than once because the environment simply fascinated me. Here plump-and-proud-of-it naked women sit on long benches in a large, steamy, mist-filled room. Children in tow, the robust women scrub little ears and backsides and shampoo each other's dark hair. Showers along the walls constantly turn on and off as women wash, gab, sweat, and shower again and again. The baths are a place to socialize and gossip, for here "the echo repeats every word thrice."

Mikkel Aaland, an expert on cultural bathing rituals and history, says Turkish baths recompensed Middle Eastern women for amusements enjoyed by proletarian European women. Historically the domain of Muslim men, they eventually became the social gathering place for wives.[1]

For Americans, whose homes include more bathtubs per capita than any other nation, bathing is most simply a ritual of necessity and at times relaxation. In contrast to global practice, Americans bathe daily, the ultimate luxury for anyone almost anywhere else in the world.

In the modest bungalow where I grew up, we children were bathed in an old-fashioned claw-foot tub. I was introduced to the rare shower in our basement where in one corner a plastic curtain created a cubicle around a wooden slatted platform. This shower was primitive and dark, but I relished the sense of my mother's pleasure while she washed her hair, then mine under gushing torrents of water.

When we moved to California, the Golden State, the bathroom in our pink stucco house held a special perk: a ceiling sunlamp where damp became dry instantaneously. Raising a family of my own, there were a variety of bathrooms, each different yet unmistakably familial. Bubble-gum-scented bubble soap and shiny Cinderella shampoo sat alongside a metal diaper pail with its Clorox odor (ah, what I would have given for a Diaper Genie!).

Today's dream bath has become the home spa, where high-end packaging is key. The French design and sophisticated fonts used on labels, nostalgic apothecary-shaped bottles and jars, and pale, whispery colors drive the market. Huge companies like Bath & Body Works and a proliferation of private online businesses cater to a woman's craving to be pampered. The bathroom, after all, is the one place where a woman is likely to think about only herself, and this is the solution to a stress-induced culture driven by Herculean expectations that a woman be there for all people at all times.

The *rest*room is the place to relieve not only our bladders but our entire bodies—of tension, strain, and fatigue. Here we can study our naked form, practice different kinds of smiles, experiment with wild hair colors or styles, lavish every inch of skin with nourishing touch, and linger away from the maddening crowd. The bath has become, most deliciously, an excuse for getting in touch with ourselves once again.

What must it have been like before the bath "room" was invented? Did the stinky ol' outhouse suffice as a place to linger just a bit? Did a woman ever get used to bathing in a galvanized kitchen tub surrounded by family? Was there a single space in her day for caressing her own face with sweet-smelling potions? Was she consigned to lugging water from the well house to soak her aching feet at the end of a grueling day?

My favorite scene in one of my favorite movies, *Places in the Heart* (starring Sally Fields), is where Edna at long last gets an opportunity to bathe at the end of a long, hot, cotton-pickin' week. Interrupted accidentally by a blind boarder, Edna is shocked, then settles nervously into the knowledge that once he hears lapping

113

of water in the tub, the embarrassment is his. What I love is the simplicity of that scene, where water itself—not a roomful of romantic products—is the heart of lavish relaxation.

One winter I had the privilege of spending an entire week with a friend who lived in a sixteenth-century cottage in Essex, England. Her home was a medieval structure through whose door I had to duck to keep from bumping my noggin. There was no central heating, only a coal fireplace in the corner of the small sitting room. So while our backsides froze, we sat in front of the fire drinking cups of tea made in a proper Royal Doulton teapot. Rain drizzled across crooked, misshapen windows. At bedtime Jane offered me her tiny chamber, once a sleeping loft, and introduced me to another Royal Doulton pot. Hand painted with an elaborate lid, it sat regally just under the bed. The pot was meant to save me the trouble of a midnight trip to the loo at "the other end of the garden."

What do you like most about your own bathroom experience? The fuzzy feel of the U-shaped rug under your bare toes on a chilly morning? The inviting lineup of pastel soaps on a pretty shelf above the sink? The feel of hot water pounding your back after a full day of work? Maybe you like saturating your clean skin with moisturizer and your clean hair with satiny conditioner.

My favorite part is tuning out the world in the rush and splash of a full-on shower. Working from a home office, I often take midday showers as a break from the shoulder and eye strain of sitting at a computer hour after hour. Sometimes I enjoy a shower just before a yoga class or before meeting a friend for dinner. At other times I shower in the morning as revitalization for another day of writing and editing or late at night to warm up before jumping into bed in a wintry cold room.

In any case, I never take bathing for granted. Surrounded by the warmth of a lovely room or in a cold-water concrete shower in a camp in the Middle East, bathing has been and will continue to be for me a special space in the day. The bathroom remains a place for me to be enchanted with my own body and a reminder of my connection to what the human race has always known—that cleanliness is relaxing and healing and that it purifies my soul as well as my flesh.

*soul*PROJECT

Relax to the Max

Nearly half of American women say their favorite mode of relaxation is bathing. Whether you do so to be proper or pampered, let's face it, nothing feels as good alone. People who prefer showers enjoy the scintillating water over shoulders and head. Bathers prefer soaking in bubbles by candlelight. How can you take relaxation by bath to the max?

- *Simply must-haves:* Fresh towels fluffed in a dryer just before bath time. A spongy, scrunchy skin cleansing pad that doubles the bubbles for soaping down. Fragrant washes in a variety of scents to tickle your fancy top to toes. A curved razor for your legs and underarms, and cream to make the blade glide. Pretty, personal toiletry bottles to inspire an aura of charm.
- *Transform the look of your bathroom with plants for a garden effect.* Plants love moisture. Experiment with different kinds and move them around until they find a place to thrive in your most personal of spaces.
- *Make room for fun.* Introduce an element of surprising décor: a trio of rubber duckies, a bouquet of fresh flowers for the weekend, a skylight over the tub, a vintage mirror instead

of a wall-sized monolith. Try an unexpected theme: cowgirls, bluesy jazz, or the whimsy of Victorian children's art. Take something fun that you just love and reproduce it over and over on the walls of your powder room paradise.

FOURTEEN

Home Office,
POSTMODERN HEARTH

Most of our lives require us to shift from place to place. As we move between home and office or between family spaces and an area designated for work in our home, our quality of speech shifts, our posture is altered, our energy level spikes with each change of environment. Each time we make such a shift, a small transformation takes place.

Clodagh

Has something been lost in our culture through high-tech innovation? Might all our digital gadgets have created a corporate community that lacks one vital ingredient—soul?

One thing is for sure: With self-employed entrepreneurs and even employees telecommuting these days, business-as-usual is being reinvented. We now access the marketplace via the Internet, and even small businesses thrive online like the shoemaker once did on Main Street. When more than 40 percent of America's energy is used for heating and cooling office buildings, home-based business makes sense for more than personal reasons. But personal reasons are key, and employees' number one complaint—lack of control over temperature levels in the work space—can be applied to other kinds of control.[1] Working from home means autonomy, self-direction, and creative responsibility for your own fortune.

The home office may be the new hearth of the postmodern family. If a home is sanctuary, the computer station may now be its symbol of essence and life, usurping the television that usurped the radio that usurped the fireside as a gathering place. Adults spend a generous amount of their personal time on PCs networking; self-educating; searching for recipes, medical diagnoses, and movie reviews; and conducting home business such as banking and shopping. Those of the dot-com generation who grew up with an intuitive sense of the Internet use it for a thousand other wild and savvy reasons. But by its nature, the Web isolates. An increasing number of people who spend at least two hours daily online are reportedly inclined toward depression. So, are the virtual technologies of home offices the flame that keeps us warm in this early second millennium or a force for further fragmentation?

The answer is complex. On the positive side, the home office makes it possible for people to be in proximity of family more hours in the day. It saves commute time and gasoline, cuts costs associated with an office wardrobe, and channels the profit back to people and not corporations. Those for whom the home office is a reality are scouring the country for "best places to live." No longer is it necessary to wait around for retirement in order to get close to nature, enjoy a small community, or be near favorite resorts. Those who negotiate the waters of technology with aplomb can make virtual realities work for rather than against them. They look less for a high standard of living and more for improved life quality.

Quality of life for me, however, has to include soul, a combination of personal history, symbol, and my intention for the future. My home office is as much sanctuary as any other room. I've positioned my mom's retro secretary desk in front of a south-facing window. A pullout keyboard drawer was the only adaptation made to the heavy L-shaped piece of furniture. But my desk is clunky compared to what designers are now calling the "non-desk," which is simply a kit of parts, adaptable to individual use. Today's virtual desktop is on the computer screen anyway. Yet I wouldn't trade my big old desk, because it rivets me to history. It's about my mother's work, surviving when the Great Depression cut funds short, and never returning to college to fulfill her dreams. For as long as I can remember, my mother sat at this desk doing bookkeeping for my dad's insurance business while raising two daughters and a son in the home where she also worked. Only recently, as an eighty-six-year-old woman, did Mother finally admit in tears, "I'll never get to go back to college." My desk is about her sacrifice.

Seated behind Mom's desk, my view is considerably different than hers was. Instead of a street lined with ranch houses, I look out at a peak of the Cascade range, Black Crater, and across a half acre studded with aspen trees. But is that more beautiful than whatever motivated her to keep going at her station day after day?

I hear her tell me pragmatically, "I sat there and worked to help pay the bills." I know what she means. Her efforts at this desk are the legacy of a time when a woman was lucky to have a job at all and when a dime for a movie was a downright luxury. She worked not for fulfillment but for daily bread. I respect this history as I value my intention to engage with work that calls me by name.

Your business is a reflection of who you are: your giftedness, character, and will. Your home office is the expression of your business. It will also express the soul you find in your work. Neither of these is static. When you make changes in a business plan, reevaluate your motivation, or experiment with the way you accessorize the office, discoveries come to light. When, in a redesign of my letterhead, I decided to reinvent my mission statement, I came up with a new direction for a second decade of independent consulting. While painting my desk white, I discovered the drawer pulls were real copper. I polished them to a golden-red patina and did away with a heavy layer of tarnish. I took this as a metaphor for my business direction. Changes in economic climate, tides of community interest, and improvements in technology are guaranteed. They affect all of us in the marketplace. Working home-based means moving in touch with change while maintaining the soul in what we do.

Occasionally someone will wonder aloud about the discipline required to run a business out of the home. Once a person is committed, the choices are simplified and that discipline becomes a way of life. The key for me has been to settle on specific office hours during which I work on one particular project. One person I know works noon to midnight, another friend works evenings and weekends, and yet another 4:00 a.m. until noon. Only occasionally do I feel the temptation to clean, cook, or make a personal call during my working day. I religiously take off weekends, a jubilant break from Monday through Friday discipline. I've noticed among home-based business owners I know that women are more likely to make it than men. Men seem to return to an office environment more quickly. Studies show that females are better at multitasking, so perhaps they handle the demands better. Or perhaps women's sense of the sacred at home and work is more integrated.

Often it is acknowledged that a professional who works out of her home can accomplish in five hours as much as the typical eight-hour employee in an office environment. If you work for yourself, you can put that extra three hours a day to work for *you*, not the corporate bottom line.

The decision of whether to work at home or at an office building is simple for me. I'd rather keep open-ended my short time on this earth than live with aggravating commutes, unending department meetings, and the distracting reality of corporate politics. By working in a home office, I've sculpted a life I love: the flexibility to hit the road for a daughter's sports event, to have coffee with a heartbroken friend, or to run an errand for my elderly mom. There are no heels, no suits, no makeup. Every day is casual, dress-down Friday.

The home office does create its own dilemmas, however. You have to plan your own appreciation days, annual bonus, and employee picnic. You are responsible for your own performance evaluation, long-term forecasts, and continuing education. You have to put together the business plan and project proposals, nail down the contracts, and do the grunt work too. You wear the hats of CEO, marketing director, creative director, production manager, public relations representative, and research assistant. The buck stops with you. Coffee and lunch breaks are optional. There are no paid vacations or sick days, health insurance, or retirement plan. But you'll never have to sit through another boring Christmas party—and every award will have your name on it!

Home-office perks abound if you look for them. Mine include deer roaming through my backyard. A doe wandered to my window one day and gazed in at me at eye level with her big brown eyes. Who needs office parties with moments like that?

I have a framed greeting card on my desk of a girl in overalls, bare feet up on her desk between her typewriter and telephone. She is chewing a straw while gazing at sunflowers out her window.

The copy reads: "We don't care how they do it in New York."[2] No, we certainly don't.

"Is this where it all happens, Marlee?" a friend of mine asked when she dropped in as I sat working. In my home office I put my soul children into words, and so it has, indeed, become my second hearth. Here are the speaker phone, the message machine, the fax, and the modem—my connections with business, while nature outside the window connects me to life itself.

Moving from living space to my home office, a transformation takes place. I become professional, goal oriented, decisive, and ambitious. But I don't expect to begin making megabucks, jet all over the world on book tours, or meet the rich and famous. I don't even want that. I am already exactly where I want to be, doing what I want to do, experiencing my own turf as a land of plenty. The home office becomes my hearth when I keep mindful of the reason I am working at all. I'm not here to create a marketable product but to fuel an authentic life.

*soul*PROJECT

Show Yourself Respect

Your home office where you go to work each day deserves high-class treatment. It should reflect your personal taste and a high level of professionalism, and promote effective work habits.

- *Organize to a T.* Think through every detail of your office needs. Familiarize yourself with office supply catalogs and stores to develop a plan for your space. Define precisely where to find what you need in a jiffy.

- *Simplify quarters.* Maintain a separate tabletop that can be cleared to set up a project. Create a bookcase for reference books, computer paper, and file holders. Designate a special drawer or cubicle for personal items separate from Post-it notes, pencils, and other office supplies. Ban knickknacks. Introduce color.

- *Label what you cannot see.* It's amazing how quickly "out of sight, out of mind" catches up with us. Label makers are not cheap, but you can't beat them for a tidy, professional appearance. If you're productive, relabel files often to accommodate increased business and more effective working styles.

- *Reinvent space.* Move things around until your office feels convenient and orderly but still suits your sensibilities. Think of ways to eradicate irritations like direct sun through a certain window or a bulletin board that you can't reach from your chair. Don't make do with irregularities; keep reinventing for an environment that serves you.

- *Don't scrimp on chairs.* A good chair is worth its weight in gold. Pick out the best one you can afford, then buy a chair one step above it. Patronize a reputable office supply and furniture store for ongoing service in case of wear and tear. You won't regret the choice.

- *Create focus.* Keep just what you need on your desk. Separate personal and business files. Hang up personal photographs on the wall or put them on a special shelf out of the way. Maintain desktop files for separate purposes; use color-coded Post-it notes or inks as reminders.

- *Declutter regularly.* Set a specific time in the week to clean your desktop and tidy your drawers. Sort small spaces during casual phone calls. Offer yourself the gift of a pleasing environment that inspires your best effort.

PART 3

The Dream Home
IN YOU

FIFTEEN

Remodeling
THE DREAM

The moment one begins dreaming-awake, a world of enticing,
unexpected possibilities opens up. A world where the ultimate
audacity becomes a reality.

Florida Donner

I dreamed I was flying through space, then put my feet down
in a landscape of rolling hills. In front of me was an old-
fashioned white country church with a tall spire. But wait! It
changed like one of those little plastic pictures in Cracker Jacks.
The church became a two-story haunted house. Tattered curtains
were blowing out the windows, and there was no sign of light
or life. The front porch and stairway were broken and sagging.
The beams barely held the roof in place. As the house changed
back into the church and then to a haunted house once more,
someone asked if I would like to go inside. I quickly said no. She

told me she would go with me, and I agreed. Together we picked our way up the broken front steps to the front door.

Inside, a large empty room stood bare except for one window to the front. Each of the other walls had a large fireplace blazing with fire. The room was warm and bright, but there was no place to sit down and enjoy it. I soon realized that was not the point. Looking down, I saw that my feet were covered with golden flames, like slippers. The person with me said, "You are wearing the shining shoes. Those shoes are going to take you somewhere."

At the time of my haunted house dream, I was frightened and lonely, shattered by a divorce I had not foreseen. I felt like the only woman alive who had experienced the humiliation of adultery and shock of abandonment. The home I had worked hard to build appeared to be crumbling away. The sanctuary I wanted our relationship to be had suddenly and dramatically changed. This dream offered hope, like finding a crumpled dollar bill in your pocket when you're on your last dime. The dream seemed to be telling me that my house was still all right on the inside. The shining shoes were a promise of moving on to good things. Nine years later I've found in that image a distinctive calling.

Change—and change is almost always the result of any forward movement—takes courage. My journey has been uphill for a long time and promises to be steeper still. Shivers of fear often make me tremble. But there are places to go. Over and over again, I quietly remind myself, *Marlee, you are wearing shining shoes.*

Since ancient times the image of feet has been a symbol of pilgrimage. Moses blessed the tribe of Asher before his death, saying, "Asher is most blessed of sons; . . . let him dip his foot in oil. Your sandals shall be iron and bronze; as your days, so shall your strength be."[1] The poet wrote that God's Word is "a lamp to my feet and a light to my path."[2] The apostle Paul reminded us of the prophetic exclamation that the feet of those who proclaim peace and bring good tidings are *beautiful*.[3] John, writing from exile, saw an angel clothed with a cloud, whose feet were like pillars of fire.[4] When I am stressed, lonely, or confused, I recall my dream of shining shoes and those biblical references referring to blessed feet—feet on a mission.

The patriarch Jacob lay his head on a stone to sleep in the wilderness after being sent on a long journey by his father. That night he dreamed of a ladder stretching from earth to heaven. Angels were going both directions on it, and the Lord stood at the top. God made a promise to Jacob about the land and the blessing that was to come through him. When Jacob woke up, he spoke these stunning words: "Surely the LORD is in this place, and I did not know it."[5]

In the most unlikely places, when we are standing before the most incredible passages of our lives, daunted by the miles ahead of us, dreams offer clues. These clues not only help us process the past; they also carry seeds of the future. Dreams are often God's way of letting us know that he is there for us.

Studying the archetypal meaning of dream images, I learned that an empty house signifies a soul-searching period or a change in personal awareness that is difficult to deal with. A derelict house is an expression that no one cares. A house in poor repair may warn of the need for renovation. Curtains blowing in the wind show inner harmony and spiritual learning, but in the case of my dream, the harmony and spirituality were literally in tatters!

I know now, like Jacob after his dream, that God was in the haunted circumstances of my life: broken heart, financial ruin, dread for what my children must endure, and much more. Since then, the image of a house has recurred in my dreams in different guises. In fact, researchers say a house is the most common setting for dreamers worldwide. Whether it be a historic mansion or a deserted shack, a house inspires exploration.

My nocturnal dreams have moved me into various kinds of homes. Usually these serve as a container for something going on in the rooms, but at least once the structure itself had the starring role. In this dream I was building a large house for which there was much to be decided and accomplished. It was a house I intended to live in. The outside looked like a classy hunting lodge. Inside, the vaulted ceiling showed off an exquisite round window of pink and red stained glass. Sightseers were taking tours through the interior, admiring it, going up and down the huge staircase. I found myself, however, walking around on the roof. It seemed there were problems in the construction process; the builder and I were trying to figure out what to do about them. I walked over to a steep sloop over the front door and looked down at the tourists coming and going . . . and then I woke up.

Researchers say dreams about a house under construction indicate a person who is self-directed. Dreams about rooftops express letting go of artificial restrictions. What a switch from my original dream many years before! I was moved by the fact that in this latter dream I was integrating the picture of the country church/haunted house. They were becoming one, my home was becoming sanctuary, both beautiful and safe. Instead of being empty, it was filled with people. That I was going to finish it and live in it, I was not in doubt.

Scientists say people who are deprived of REM sleep—when dreams are more visual in content—are prone to irritability, fatigue, memory loss, and poor concentration. Clearly, the Creator has beautifully designed our unconscious. It is meant not to torment us with bizarre visions or leave us vulnerable but to give us a way to work toward a healthier waking life. Dream time helps us recognize important truths about ourselves and our surroundings. They cooperate with our "day" dreams as raw material with which to improve our lives. We are dreaming all the time, Carl Jung believed. Only the distractions of waking life leave us unaware of that fact, he noted.[6]

Like a house, my life has several levels (or stories) and many rooms divided into public and private spaces. As I bring significance from night dreams or private spaces into my waking life or public places, I remodel my dream home on an ongoing basis. After that first haunted house dream, I began to invest my dreams with regard, recording them first thing in the morning. I let them simmer on the back burner of my mind, hoping eventually to read between the lines of their strange pictures. One thing that facilitated this was sharing dreams on a regular basis with two friends. We not only laughed a lot but also found that when you share dreams, you can't hide anything from one another. We began to see important truths in each other's dreams that escaped the dreamer's own perception. The most eccentric dream could turn out to be the most insightful.

When I have an utterly ridiculous dream, an erotic dream, or a dangerous dream, I'm tempted not to document it. Through the years, however, I've discovered that the dreams that intimidate me most are the most useful—that is, if I'm willing to explore their territory and understand the questions they ask of me.

My recurring nightmares often involve houses, usually temporary lodging in foreign countries and strange landscapes. Almost always I am lost, alone, and late—for a taxi, a bus, or an airplane. Attempting to leave some place where I'm staying, I'm mired down in packing too much stuff into too few suitcases. Having traveled a lot and moved many times, I am tempted to see these bad dreams as my soul wrestling with its baggage. Or perhaps I fear deep down that I'm going to be too late to show up for my own life. Working with these themes, my dream-group friends challenged me to actually change the dreams. They said no one should have to lug around that much stuff! Starting with my closets, I've begun to lighten the load in a concrete way. I cast off whatever has had its day. Surprisingly, the dreams have begun to dissipate.

All but one, that is—a daydream. A recurring daydream of mine is to build on to my house a prayer turret that rises above the roofline. Through a circle of windows, I want to look upon treetops toward the mountains while spending time with God. Looking deeper, I've wondered, *What might I learn from this dream?*

Research informs me that commonly a castle or turret image indicates a longing for security. It may signify that the strength of my own defenses is isolating me from others. Both these ideas fit, and I'm looking to change. Worn excuses—I don't have enough money, education, or the right kind of personality to accomplish my dreams—are no longer viable. I reach out to other people and stand on the promises of El Shaddai, the Provider. This dream is a big improvement over one I had years ago of hiding under my desk to get away from a houseful of noisy, demanding teenagers.

I'm climbing higher and expecting more. The shining shoes are taking me somewhere I've never dreamed of going.

What about your dream home?

You are creating it from the stuff you own about yourself— what you allow to surface in your consciousness. Dream homes are built from the brick of what you accept, tolerate, and concede to. They are built of the stuff you celebrate and the stuff you fear. They are built of what you honor and of all the reasons you party! Each of us is summoned to build and inhabit our dream home, God's design for, and calling upon, our lives.

"In My Father's house are many mansions," Jesus said.[7]

Why wouldn't he involve us in the joy of helping to build them, starting right here on earth? Brick by brick we shape God's flamboyant vision of the kingdom. We spread the mortar stone upon precious stone—jasper, sapphire, emerald, topaz, amethyst—studded with pearls.[8] Now that is a dream house!

soul PROJECT

House-a-Home Dream Images

Dreams are a conversation with oneself, a dialogue of symbols and images that takes place between the unconscious and conscious levels of the mind," says David Fontana.[9] For those who wish to enrich their dream life, the following list of symbols around the idea of house or home may help.[10]

- *Windows.* Your ability to understand the outside world or to transcend your own understanding about a particular topic, sometimes believed to be feminine symbols.
- *Doors.* Your need to be more accessible to yourself or to others. A locked door signifies you are in need of the key to an issue or problem or that you are finding it difficult to express emotions. A closed door represents despair or indecision. Open doors invite you to explore possibilities. A threshold indicates you are about to embark on a new and exciting venture.
- *Rooms or floors.* Various aspects of your personality or mind. Living rooms signify your waking life. Upper rooms signify your spirituality, goals, and aspirations.
- *Cramped rooms.* You would like to enjoy life more but feel overwhelmed by responsibility and obligations.
- *Cluttered rooms.* You need to lighten your load or simplify your life.
- *Sparsely furnished rooms.* You feel unsupported, lack physical or emotional comfort, or both.
- *Stairs leading nowhere.* You are at a loss in a relationship or otherwise.

- *A clean house.* You are ready for new challenges.
- *A dirty house.* You are overdue for a rest. Whew!
- *Basement or cellar.* You are working with an issue you may not even be aware of, or you fear someone will discover your secrets.
- *A tall house.* Your potential is only just being tapped.
- *A small house.* You are wrestling with doubts.
- *Bathroom.* You are trying to eliminate something unnecessary or unpleasant from your life, or you feel vulnerable.
- *Halls and corridors.* You need to get in touch with deep-seated uncertainty.
- *Walls.* There are obstacles and restrictions in your life that you need to deal with.
- *Rooftop.* You are releasing restrictions.
- *A locked gate.* You're being stubborn; take another look.
- *An open gate.* Accept what is open to you.

SIXTEEN

Dollhouses:
DREAMS IN MINIATURE

Perhaps a new simplicity will lie in clarity about what it is we want, and what we need, from the rooms of our lives.

Dominique Browning

t is my first day of kindergarten. I see something I'd only dreamed of: a dollhouse filled with accessories. I kneel down and start to play with it, putting baby in the cradle, moving mother to the kitchen, seating father in the armchair. I imagine my someday self in my someday home. My heart is filled with delight—ecstasy, really. I had poured over the dollhouses in the Sears and Roebuck Wish Book, but now for the first time, I wrap my chubby fingers around a tiny piano and miniature mother. Another child sits down beside me, putting her hands inside the house to move things around. I shrink back, startled and bewildered. I start to cry. The teacher calls my mother, suggesting I'm not ready to start school. I end up at home watching another year's worth of *I Love Lucy* on daytime TV.

What did *I* want? I was never encouraged to say by that teacher or any other. I never had a dollhouse to play with, so perhaps that is why I developed a complex inner world instead. Rather than the wholesome simplicity of knowing what I want and need from the rooms of my life,[1] a labyrinth of dramatic dreamscapes began to take shape that still mystify even me. Imaginary friends came to play in my intriguing inner rooms. My little people, miniature versions of myself, had all the mixed adorability and orneriness of Mary Norton's characters in *The Borrowers*—they were imbued with enigmatic soul. The architecture in which they frolicked was many layered and multidimensional—not the square rooms of an ordinary two-story, cutaway dollhouse. I was looking for something. The dollhouse in my mind took on a life of its own.

More than half a lifetime later, I am still exploring that. But I am looking for a new simplicity. I want to play, at last, with the dollhouse of my dreams.

This seems to be true for many women of a certain age. The world of dollhouses and miniatures reemerged in the early 1970s as a popular hobby that boomed into a huge business. The International Miniatures Artisans Guild was created to promote it as an art form. Eventually the IMAG added bylaws, started a lecture series and demonstrations, and then sponsored a major exhibit in the rotunda of the Museum of the City of New York.

If you read through numerous chat rooms, you'll find it obvious that there is something more going on with dollhouse enthusiasts than just a recreational pastime. One woman commented that her favorite thing is to arrange everything just right inside her dollhouse, then close it up and peep through the windows like a giant. Another contributor said she was given—in her thirties—a dollhouse by her parents and was thriving in decorating it. An entire chat room is composed of conversation from the viewpoint of the dolls: "By the way," wrote one, "I hope you don't mind people with disabilities, but I can't bend my legs. Please tell me that I'm not alone in this."

At Tiny Talk, a chat room whose motto is "Wee scale the world," you'll find workshops on making miniature stained-glass windows and French tapestries. Photos abound of "room boxes" that include such fantastical themes as Geppetto's workshop, a Gothic mystery mansion, and an Edwardian greenhouse. Some dollhouse enthusiasts spend a lot of money on their creations. One woman captured the ambience of a tiny hilltop village in France she visited with her daughter. Another made a replica of a sixty-eight-room mansion she had seen on her travels. The creator of a six-foot-long dream house with no fewer than five bedrooms confided, "I love to make beds!" Others, with just as much creative spirit, enjoy creating furniture and accessories out of ordinary household objects like milk bottle caps and toothpaste lids turned into tiny tables and chairs. The feeling seems to be that most dollhouse lovers just plain enjoy designing and crafting small, beautiful things. This was true of my middle daughter who once scooped up a handful of wet clay along the historic Oregon Trail. She sculpted several tiny heads, each with a different expression—her tribute to the pioneers. At home she fashioned bodies for these clay dolls out of cotton batting and fabric scraps for her dollhouse.

I believe that somehow this fascination with dollhouses is a way to arrive at what we want and what we need from the rooms of our lives—in a dream home designed especially with that in mind. Sheila Davis of Portland, Oregon, says God used a dollhouse to help her process the death of her husband to cancer in midlife. "I came to understand after he died that our house was going to be used for different purposes," she says. She began a process of remodeling and redecorating her own home, starting with their bedroom. Davis saw the renovation of her home as synonymous with renovation of her own spirit as she adjusted to being alone. "Parting with some things, I realized there is room for the new," she told me. "I began cleaning out the old in my soul as well, including wounds and hurts that weren't yet healed."

Davis was led to purchase a dollhouse and place it in her living room as a way to make even more visible the changes in her own life. She is decorating it little by little, starting with the bedroom, as she moves through grief. She uses her dollhouse to minister to other women as she speaks across the city, and she has even taken it to the state prison women's facility as an object lesson to demonstrate rebuilding one's life.

If you were a dollhouse, what would you look like? Would you be art nouveau with Tiffany windows? A Victorian mansion? A Japanese teahouse? Perhaps you'd be a toadstool residence for pixies. Why not? There is plenty of room for eccentricities: one online browser said she was creating a dollhouse for cat lovers; another, a sixties-era Hell's Angels club. Both were asking for advice and exchanging tips to create just the right look.

Not all of us are perfectionists—we just want to find a place of our own. A friend's childhood dollhouse was assembled by gluing shoe boxes on top of each other. Her mother decorated them with wallpaper samples. Windows were made from pictures of landscapes cut from magazines, glued to inside walls, and framed with Popsicle sticks. Another friend was lucky enough to have a father who built her a dollhouse from an orange crate into which he cut a door and windows. Her grandmother contributed scraps of drapery fabric and carpet. My children's friends had Barbie Dream Houses more lavish than any home. Today a Laura Ashley dollhouse is available for which "children are the designers." Based on the romantic floral designs of the British designer, it features changeable wallpaper, working lights, and the crackling sounds of a fireplace!

However your dollhouse looked, what matters is how you explore in the rooms of your life today the dreams envisioned in that miniature world. Playing out your gifts in a home—and any home is a dream home—is the most enchanting work of all. It is a kind of hallowed drama in which the child in you finds out who she is and what she wants. Home and garden magazines may still focus on the ideal, but in reality, the concept of home is not so much a style statement as a mission statement.[2] Nothing is ever perfect. Life comes to us in great big doses as Sheila Davis experienced. It also comes in dribs and drabs. It is not always pretty. It does not always smell holy.

It seems to me that dream houses are about whatever makes you say life is good—anyway. One survivor of the Oregon Trail pronounced that to be true when she planted a rosebush beside her one-room cabin in the fertile Willamette Valley. She had dumped her antique mahogany dresser in a ravine somewhere. Her mother's Queen Anne chairs had been left long before on a dusty trail in Wyoming. Her youngest child had died of typhoid in Idaho, and a brother had drowned while crossing the Columbia River. But this resilient mother had carried a rosebush across prairies and mountains to the Pacific Northwest and went to work playing dream house by planting it. Yellow roses blossomed the following summer.

My grandmother set up house again and again in the scorched Kansas landscape with four small sons. She found a way to make peace with the losses of the Dust Bowl, including the death of a fifth son who lived only two days. She found a way to get what she wanted from the rooms of her life. The economic downturn of our own time, more than seventy years later, surprised many who lost their beautiful homes and life savings. People have been reexamining their values since the tragedy of 9/11 rocked us. In the wake, we are redefining home. We are finding dollhouse dreams still in place. We cut back and scale down and relearn what we once knew playing with dollhouses. Dream homes cannot be defined by square footage or the cost of the furnishings. Dream homes are about imbuing the place you live with a sense of place—and knowing that is where the party is happening.

Years ago I built a Victorian dollhouse from a kit, working after my middle daughter's bedtime each night for months. I glued together the foundation and each wall, and set in place each window and wooden shake shingle. After carefully applying gingerbread trim, I painted it pink and white. Come Christmas day, my daughter's job was to decide what she wanted from each room, a labor of concentrated absorption. She made a hand-stitched family: a mother and father, several sisters, a brother and baby, as well as a grandma and grandpa. Today that dollhouse is dilapidated from a lot of touching by small hands.

I know a lot of people who live in modest homes and scrimp from one paycheck to the next. I also know those who live in fabulous palaces and a never-never land of abundance. Yet in reality, each of us lives moment to moment. Like the pioneer woman with the yellow rosebush, all we can carry in our hands is this moment. Certainly hopes get tangled up with losses, but dollhouse dreams teach us to look for something beautiful that can be made of remnants. Dollhouses teach that hope and promise, not opulence and embellishment, need to be reenacted again and again in the rooms of our lives.

Little girls know intuitively what grown-ups seldom admit: The "good" life doesn't come from accumulating things; it comes in expressing your own mystique. The home of your dreams is not about how much you spend but about how magnificent you are.

soul PROJECT

Envision a
Sugarplum Ranch

When my family moved to a land of bright orange fruit with mountains on one side and the Pacific Ocean on the other, the world changed to Technicolor. Our new home was a pink stucco house with white wood trim, and like Clara's dream of the sugarplum fairy, my memory of that home is sunshiny iridescent. I was eight years old, a middle child with a romantic imagination.

In my own backyard, three acres of luscious Elephant Heart plums hung low during harvest. They introduced me to the fragrant scent I have forever after identified with summer. A grove of pecans provided its autumn free fall for holiday pies. Citrus trees offered magnificent globes of juice in what Southern Californians call "winter."

You might say the pink house was like a scene from the old TV show *Lassie*. It was there I romped with a collie puppy named Lucky and a coal-black, long-haired kitty. It was there I first heard the ethnic smatterings of a foreign language spoken by the migrant workers my father hired as pickers. But nothing surpassed my delight with the irrigation canals that curved through our property. My brother and I built Indian villages along them. We constructed twig teepees and wood-chip wagon-train camps alongside the "river" and navigated plastic boats through its twists and turns.

But during the last of those wonder years, developers of hurry-up housing sliced away everything green in a radius around us. We watched as Caterpillars leveled hillsides, replacing them with sidewalks and sewer systems. Our isolated plum orchard became a hangout for teenagers and a depository of trash. The pink house served as a sweet oasis for the closing chapter of childhood, but I grieved as it was annexed to the city. That same year I left childhood as well.

It wasn't until my own middle daughter, at age twelve, opened her romantic imagination to me that I began to see a pattern to all of life's changes and to accept them as grace itself. "Things are always changing, Marmie," my daughter Leyah would say in our bedside talks while the darkness whispered. "Maybe, if I don't like the way they are today, I'll just wait until tomorrow."

I think of the pink house now as my daughters go into the world. The oldest is buying her first home, the youngest is moving into a college dorm, and the middle daughter is starting her first job in New York City. Alone in my home for the first time in twenty-five years, I realize that things have never stopped changing. I can't hold back the dynamic of life any more than I could hold back 1950s suburban sprawl. The pain of it is bittersweet. I savored my season of sunshine and fruitfulness. The sugarplum house remains, like my memories of pink-bundled baby girls, plum good.

What sweetness of the past in your home do you treasure? Make a list of moments. Write a poem about one, or compose a letter to the room where a memory was made. Write about the good things that happened there and the changes that have taken place over the years. If you're a more visual person, take pictures of architectural features in your home. Look for the way light is seen through the lens, and hunt for interesting angles and lines or perspectives. Shoot upward from the floor or downward from atop a ladder. Note one memory on the back of each picture. Frame and display the pictures in a grouping or put them in a scrapbook you call *My House of Dreams*. Tuck this in a place where you keep treasures.

SEVENTEEN

Finding Your Tribe:
THE NOMAD IN YOU

The circumstances of fly-fishing—the spectacular and ferocious beauty of the landscape, the awesome power of nature—were as much something to catch sight of as the wild flashes of silver were something to catch hold of. The most we can do, I think, is put ourselves in their path.

Page Hill Starzinger

Frank Lloyd Wright is known for his refusal to design any house isolated from its natural setting. Spending summers on his uncle's farm in Wisconsin, he grew up conscious of the healing power of nature and its importance to the integrity of our lives and homes. In an age of overdevelopment in which builders cram houses anywhere there is a space, it would be good to look back at habitats that have incorporated the reality for which Wright simply took the credit. Certain people groups have always translated the emotion and sensory beauty of their surroundings into their homes, making them intimate spaces, not showplaces.

Native Americans made this sensibility their business when crafting living quarters for a family or a village for the tribe. Using raw materials from their environment, northern Inuits found a way to create shelter that not only protected them *from* the blasts of frigid moisture moving through their wild habitat but were constructed *of* it. When darkness dominates three seasons of the year, ice crystallizes on nearly every surface, and the Inuits took advantage of this. Their homes, known as igloos, meaning "snow houses," were formed by stacking blocks of ice in the shape of a dome. Actually a cluster of several open spaces or rooms, igloos were sometimes connected to neighbors' homes by long straight tunnels under the snow. As the igloo took shape, blocks of snow or ice were shaved slightly to curve inward until a small dome was formed. As building blocks were put in place, their edges were banged, causing snow to melt then quickly refreeze. This process fused joints tightly together. Later, snow was packed against the sides using wooden shovels.[1]

The igloo has captured our imagination. Capitalizing on that, entrepreneurs at www.eskimold.com want to sell you a patent-pending mold designed to produce perfect-shaped blocks of snow to build igloos for your family and neighbors. Although it took a native man and woman about an hour to build one, even with the molds, you might want to count on a little more time! If you don't want to build your own, the Ice Hotel near Quebec City, Canada, offers lodging rebuilt each winter of 11,000 tons of snow and 350 tons of ice. Bedrooms boast eighteen-foot ceilings, fireplaces, hot tubs, and furniture carved from ice blocks, all to be enjoyed at a "cozy" room temperature of 28 degrees Fahrenheit. Deer pelts will keep you and your honey warm after your "white wedding" in the hotel's cathedral, where colossal arches filter sunlight through ice. What better way to integrate nature into happily-ever-aftering?[2]

How wonderfully, eccentrically odd that preindustrial peoples chose to protect themselves from ice by burrowing into its protective layer. How appropriate that the dream homes of the Inuits are built of the very stuff that threatens them. How beguiling that the ingenuity of humankind has allowed us to create life-affirming comfort from the raw material of distress. How beautiful that native peoples like the Inuits have not only embraced difficulty but transcended it, finding ways to transform nature's power for pain into potent strength, creating from the formidable threat of ice and snow a sensuous sanctuary.

Natives around the Great Lakes and eastward were equally adept at building their homes out of local resources. A wigwam is a movable hut built with an arched framework of poles and overlaid with bark or rush mats. On the Great Plains, the early Americans fashioned tepees from poles wrapped with smoked buffalo hides. Usually built by the women, these cone-shaped tents included an inner lining to force air circulation and allow smoke to escape. The teepees were often angled steeper on one side to brace against the wind and sewn together with animal sinew, then decorated with occasional paintings of hunts or tribal rituals. Flexible and rain resistant, they could be quickly dissembled and dragged by dogs or horses as the tribe migrated with the herds.

How many variations of teepees did I try to build—in miniature or life size—as a little girl? I don't remember being highly successful, but, oh, the wigwams and tepees of my imagination! The leathery aroma of soft animal skins. The sweet scent of mats woven of plains grasses. The colors emerging as the hide was embellished with beads, shells, and stones. The rugged canopy under which I snuggled by starlight in my dreams. By day, I hovered over clay pots simmering over a fire of buffalo dung. I raised rambunctious little ones, braiding long dark hair into tightly woven patterns, finished off with leather ties and feathers.

However we compare our romantic idealizations of nomadic life against grim realities, the mystery remains. There was peace and war, laughter and lovemaking, hard work and incessant searching for food over long distances, but the center of life was the shelter where the idea of sacrifice, the shed blood of animals, and the bounty of those animals brings to mind the idea of holy ground. Holy, because it is about where we live, our dream of life, our hopes and fears and place in history. Holy, because it integrates the complex relationship between climate, land forms, plants, sociological realities, and humankind's spiritual environment.

In modern times we imitate the migratory patterns of Native Americans by living for short periods in tents, campers, or motor homes. On occasion we sleep under the open sky. Alternative lifestyles promote portable domed yurts, inspired by those still in use among indigenous people on the high plains of Central Asia. Drum tight, wind resistant, and leak proof, these provide an option for hearty souls looking for simplicity and affordability. Although yurts are gentle on the planet, it is unlikely that a yurt frenzy will surge across the nation. Most Americans still dream of a cabana in the Bahamas, a garden plot in California's foothills, or a chic apartment in Paris. Some may settle for a log cabin hideaway in the Rockies, an adobe hacienda in Mexico, or a renovated loft in Manhattan. But whether we live in a huge ranch house in Texas or a townhouse in Miami, aren't we all just camping on this earth? As pilgrims, we're temporary residents on the globe. No matter what we accumulate and cart around from place to place, our time to enjoy it will be shorter than we think.

Perhaps indigenous peoples knew better. They somehow knew that a dream home is wherever the tides or herds take us, close to family, in connection with community. America is still a nomadic society, but in contrast to our Native American countrymen, these days we migrate alone, isolated, and often out of context with any heritage whatsoever. We travel linearly while the early Americans saw that everything comes full circle like the seasons. They lived in circular homes and arranged their villages in circles, promoting protection and belonging. We build rectangular houses surrounded by high fences on straight streets. Blended into one homogenous nation, many Americans have lost a sense of legacy and security—the sort that cannot be purchased. While native peoples, traveling in tribes, took theirs with them, we leave ours behind.

Nomadic shelters of long ago implied spiritual healing inherent to living in harmony with nature. These shelters were wonderful examples of the maxim "Live simply so that others may simply live." Weathered faces and clothing detailed with ornaments from the wild fed a sense of integrity and beauty that we miss today in a world of face-lifts and plunging necklines. But many of us have gone absent, and we are seeking our tribe.

We long to live interdependently, creating intimate spaces, not showplaces. One day we will wake up to the fact that we need each other after all. Perhaps then the fences constructed between us and our habitats will come down. Guided by our soul hunger, we may yet create a new paradigm for our neighborhoods limited only by our resourcefulness or our fear.

These ideas have brought me to a revolutionary decision. Basking in dreams of renovating and remodeling my house, I envisioned its glory. There was to be a new porcelain sink with a stylish kitchen faucet. A garden bathroom would replace the dated cubby that offers barely enough room to stand between toilet, tub, and vanity. Pine plank floors, weathered to a fine patina, would replace the worn carpet. Dancing would happen nightly when the earthy, colorful wool rugs were rolled to the side. I could hardly wait to get started. Then, as if awakening from a sweet dream to brutal reality, I realized that dream no longer fit the terrain of my life. The buffalo herds have moved on. With my children grown and gone, the teepee no longer includes gathering with people to whom I belong. The structure no longer holds any allure. I have friends, of course, along with activities that have my name written all over them. But the tribe calls.

Only a grandmother will recognize the drama of my unexpected epiphany. My granddaughter, one hundred miles to the west, is a toddler and will soon be in school. I don't want to miss her. I want to be part of her life. So I've decided to move and am settling at least temporarily where Mira's mom and dad promise all the babysitting I can stand. My dream home must fit the landscape. So I'll rent my cottage home and relocate just across the mountains.

An igloo? A wigwam? A tepee? A simple, staid duplex just around the corner from a blue-eyed cherub with curly hair?

I no longer give lip service to the most charming home anywhere on earth. I want to be smack-dab where my heart is. Shaping a dream home vision is about going where the fish are jumping. Can you catch sight of them? Can you catch hold of them?

I'm going to at least put myself in their path.

soul PROJECT

Create Your Dream Home Collage

You want to make your home a personal expression of you: your preferences, your history, and the legacy you want to leave. Do you know where to start? Perhaps you have not yet recognized and owned your own preferences or your own past. Or perhaps you are unsure how to express those in your décor.

Why not start by creating on paper a visual of your dream home? A paper collage may help you create the environment that expresses who you are and what you want. Follow these steps:

- *Collect a stack of magazines to cut up.* You may be able to get outdated issues free at the library, at thrift stores, or in the recycle bin.
- *Gather family photographs that you can use for this project.*
- *Secure a large piece of poster board and a set of colored pens, pencils, pastels, or paints.*
- *Keep scissors and a glue stick handy.* You may want to use supplies that add texture to the collage, such as sequins, glitter, trims, natural materials like leaves from the trees around your house, flower petals, shells, or anything else that evokes what "dream home" means to you.
- *Work on a large table where you can spread out your supplies.* Set aside at least one hour when you don't have to look at the clock.
- *Cut out images that strike your fancy.* You may want to use just a portion of a picture or a particular detail. Work quickly, then sort those that strike you as particularly personal. Start to arrange the pictures on the poster board, working from

the center. Cut around pictures or use just the parts that speak to you.

- *Settle on an intriguing center point for your collage.* Use a photo of yourself in the center or a symbol of yourself or something three-dimensional—a seashell, a strong but rusty nail, or a beautiful leaf.

- *Think about the feelings the images evoke.* Label the feelings with pen, cut out words or letters from a magazine, use rub-on letters (from a stationery store), express feelings with color. Your completed collage should match in mood the way you want your home to make others and yourself feel. When you look at the collage, you should feel those feelings.

- *Let the collage evolve.* Paste over anything you decide you don't like, or use color washes over images to "ghost" them back or fade them. Work in bits of magazine articles, receipts for household items, ticket stubs, quotes, or photos of your family.

- *Keep working until you get the look and feel you want.* Look for themes emerging, such as "Home is where the heart is" or "One spot of enchantment." Create a sense of history alongside your intentions and your dreams for your home by the images you choose.

- *Place this collage in a place where you will see it every day.* (I keep mine on the back wall of my walk-in closet above the shirt rack.) Use it to inspire you toward creating your personal look and feel in the rooms of your home.

EIGHTEEN

A Tree House
TAKES A BOUGH

To be rooted is perhaps the most important and least recognized need of the human soul.

Simone Weil

Since Disneyland opened its gates in 1955, I've made many trips to the Magic Kingdom. Countless hours of my childhood were spent waiting for popular E-ticket rides. But there's no disputing that my all-time favorite attraction was the B-ticket Swiss Family Robinson tree house. A tribute to the ingenuity of fictitious characters popularized by the 1960 movie, the tree house celebrates and romanticizes family togetherness. A little girl could lose herself climbing up, up, up an intricate series of footbridges into a banyan tree to the lilt of whimsical calliope music. Rooms seemed to be integrated at random into the seventy-foot-high, ninety-foot-diameter tree house. All the while, bamboo buckets on pulleys, clicking in rhythmical cadence, raised two hundred gallons of water per hour through a labyrinth of branches. Remnants of furniture and artifacts salvaged from the legendary shipwreck had been fashioned into functional necessities. These made for beautifully detailed décor—like the huge conch shell that became a sink. Traipsing up the tree house's sixty-eight steps, and down the next sixty-nine, I took my time observing how a tree became a home.

What made me feel like I belonged to this tree house as much as to any place I'd ever lived?

I remembered the movie dialogue, where Herr Robinson said to his wife who was not happy with the prospect of keeping house among leaves and figs, "The world is full of nice ordinary little people who live in nice ordinary little houses on the ground." Then he asked her, "Didn't you ever dream of a house in the trees?"

I have. Isn't the tree-house dream house universal? That assumption is validated by the success of the 1813 book by Swiss pastor Johann David Wyss about the shipwrecked clan. Many of us have spent at least one night under a starry sky in a homemade shack perched in the branches of a tree. The beat goes on, for tree-house resorts and communities around the globe are popular. You'll find them along the Mediterranean coast in Turkey; on the Hawaiian and Fiji islands; in North Queensland, Australia; and on both coasts of the United States. In these locales you'll find accommodation suspended between heaven and earth that ranges from five-star luxury to a rustic room for two—with a chamber pot under the bed.

I've never heard a sermon on the probability, but I like to think of Adam and Eve as living in a tree house. I imagine Eve to be a lot like me. If I lived in a garden and got to go around naked and unashamed all the time, I'd want a romantic nest, wouldn't you? Give me stars twinkling through leafy boughs each night, fresh breezes rocking my cradle in the sky, and dewdrops awakening me with kisses in the morning.

Adam, of course, had missed the universal boyhood fun of building forts and tree houses in his own backyard. I think of him, virile and full of creative notions, seeking just the right tree for a honeymoon habitat. I'm sure it had southern exposure, with wide leaves for protection from the elements and pink blossoms in May. In my fantasy, Adam carved an adult-sized cradle in a giant branch with just enough room to curl up in the arms of his beloved. Padding it with sheep's wooly fleece and perfumed flower petals, Adam would later carve another niche for their son Cain and then another for Abel. If they'd never been banished from the garden, by the time the world's first couple held great-grandkids on their knees, the old homestead would have been as comfy as a well-worn park bench.

Perhaps an entire community of Genesis families eventually made their homes in treetops. Perhaps they became expert climbers like the Korowai people of Indonesia who live in houses up to 150 feet in the air.

For a Western and slightly more modern version of treetop living, you'll find Treesort, a resort in the tree-studded state of Oregon that is a summer camp for families. The resort offers lodging in Cabintree, Treezebo, Forestree, the Schoolhouse Suite, or the Peacock Perch. The only camp rule is that while living in a tree you're responsible to "make yourself at home." The Tree House Institute of Arts and Culture, founded by Treesort's entrepreneur, is the only place in the world that offers vocational instruction in engineering, design, and construction for building tree houses.

So there you have it—no excuse not to live life out on a limb.

Another innovative fellow on the other side of the country was just as eager to branch into the tree-house philosophy. He built the first accessible tree-house prototype for the physically challenged. Forever Young sits solidly atop twenty-one trees in Vermont, with six of those growing right through the middle of its living space. Envisioned as a camp for kids with cancer, the house includes twenty-four screened windows looking out on Lake Champlain. As a place where kids can feel normal for a week, Forever Young is designed to facilitate emotional relaxation away from the trauma of terminal disease and a hospital environment.

"It used to be kid stuff," writes *Smithsonian* magazine's Suki Casanave, "but these days more and more adults are building in trees to get high."[1] If not to get high, then at least to seek emotional or spiritual restoration. I know of a two-story "tree" house whose bedroom windows are embraced on two sides by the swaying branches of huge pines. Ponderosa needles rustle in the wind against the glass as desert stars glow through. This is a retreat designed for nurturing womblike space that, I believe, may serve to heal childhood wounds of abuse and maternal neglect.

Don't we all need this in some way?

As Casanave says, anybody may discover the joys of arboreal hideaways. If you can't build your own right now, you can browse through best-selling books, attend exhibitions, or enroll in a workshop. Online, a multitude of builders offer plans, practical tips, and photographs. One of these, Jonathan Fairoaks, says trees are dynamic organisms that deserve love and attention. He adds, "The tree is the actual architect. You learn to interpret its plans."[2] Every tree house that has ever been constructed takes on a life of its own, because each tree is as individual as you and me.

The Bible is full of powerful references about trees from the first chapter of Genesis to the last chapter of Revelation. Right in the middle, the book of Proverbs declares Wisdom, a female archetype, to be a tree of life to those who take hold of her.[3]

Surrounded on all sides by trees in my own home, I've wondered what it takes to survive hundreds or thousands of years like one: *What great wisdom would time produce in my trunk, like sap in the very veins of me?*

Unlike you and me, trees never stop growing. What better metaphor for survival and wisdom? Until their demise, a tree's roots are an earth machine operating continuously in the dark and damp. As the fastest-growing part of a tree, they grow more branches and longer branches than the visible trunk. A tree's roots serve as a mighty anchor to hold itself upright, but the pearly white hairs, fine as a spider's thread, that shoot from them, are the chief water-collecting mechanism. Wherever there is moisture, they appear suddenly, pushing themselves between soil particles. A root hair will flatten when it finds a film of moisture, then wrap itself around the particle to suck up the water, sending it up the trunk to the leaves. A full-grown apple tree lifts about four gallons of water each hour! In such a perfect ecosystem, chlorophyll, acting with the power of sunlight on leaves, turns the moisture's salts into plant food. That flows back just beneath the bark to feed every living cell in the tree.

Even when trees die, the so-called "snags" are as necessary to the environment as living trees. Valued as habitat for a host of wildlife, snags are never removed from the scene by the forest service. Nature shows that even burned-out timber is intertwined and interdependent with living things, so a tree never outgrows its resourcefulness. It stands tall, reaches upward, and stays useful just by being there.

The more I've reflected on the nature of trees, the more this concept has helped me through rough times. My time spent thinking about trees has taken me from wanting to escape to a tree house somewhere far away to wanting to become one myself.

I vow to think in lofty ways and stretch horizontally as far as I can, touching others around me. I am flexible in hard times and want to stand in a forest of mutual support and community. I hope music will be heard from the canopy of my life. Will it be the warbles and whistles of meadowlarks or the screeching of a blue jay? Maybe an artist will sit at my foot and paint a picture of me with fanciful bird cottages in my hair. Perhaps a freckled child will climb my branches and leave a mailbox for notes to and from woodland sprites.

Everybody needs a habitat, and I'd like to offer strong boughs for people who need a place to nest. Climb into my arms. Curl up in my shade. Tickle my feet with tulips and dandelions.

The poet Shel Silverstein said what I want most—to be a "cozy as can be house."[4] Let it start right here, right now.

soul PROJECT

Tap into the Power of Plants

Transform any room in your house with green, growing things. Bedrooms and a home office especially welcome interestingly patterned leaves that give off oxygen. Plants are mesmerizing because they have a tendency to do surprising things. They survive when you least expect it (and, yes, can die when you try very hard to save them) and twist toward the light in enigmatic ways or catch a breeze through a window and nod in the glory of it.

Plants provide personality and life. Just a little bit of knowledge is all you need, the kind you can chat about with the plant salesperson at your local greenhouse.

Get plants that set your fancy to whirling. Read up on anything exotic or fragile looking. Gather specific tips for specific plants on the Internet. That's also a place you can get all the advice you need on feeding and watering, containers, light, and pest control. You'll have best results if you buy plants with groupings in mind; they love fellowship just like you and I do.

I have a house full of plants that I know nothing about. If they don't thrive, I move them around until they do. If they still wilt, I try not to take it personally. The worst thing I've ever done to any of my plants is overwater. Occasionally they forgive me. When they don't, I forgive them. I tolerate only low-maintenance plants, pets, and kids—they know it and seem to like me anyway.

Oh, and by the way, I promise they grow beautifully to the music of Norah Jones.

NINETEEN

A Cave Dweller's
PENTHOUSE PARADOX

If your everyday life appears to be unworthy subject matter, do not complain to life. Complain to yourself. Lament that you are not poet enough to call up its wealth.

Rainer Maria Rilke

A caterpillar waiting inside a cocoon. A seed buried in the ground. An embryo growing inside a womb. Saint Perpetua writing from a dark prison. Helen Keller surviving then thriving in her mute, inky world. Each of these examples tells a tale from the shadows.

I think about these images as I snuggle deep under covers, lost to the world for an entire week. I am weak with the flu, cranky and weighted down. I think, *I should be feeling better, get back to work, back to the gym. I should walk the dog, clean the house, communicate with friends and family.* My body doesn't respond. I am unable to lift my head to drink water or look out the window. I envision the pile of paperwork on my desk and the answering machine crammed with calls. I have past-due bills to pay and deadlines to meet—always deadlines. But my body asks—no, my body demands—more cave time.

I lie in bed and wonder about cave dwellings. Contra the tree houses imagined in the garden in the preceding chapter, subterranean shelters are humankind's earliest lodgings. They speak of animated life in the shadows. They have something to teach me of the human condition. If a wildflower can grow out of rock, as evident in the lava fields of the Cascade Mountains I hike, then something lovely can grow from any cavernous physical or emotional abyss.

Nature's recesses have always offered shelter that by virtue of human presence becomes not only livable but transformative. Fascination with the mystery of underground places has become a popular hobby too. People who enjoy crawling on their bellies through cold, wet passageways and squeezing through jagged, wet openings have their very own magazine even. No doubt there are some spiritual analogies here, but cavers disavow them. They claim to explore earth's tunneled wilderness simply for the thrill of discovery. "Cave softly," they say, "these are fragile things."[1]

Formed as rain and time combine over thousands of years, caves are the only shelters in certain climates that guarantee survival. Weather, wild animals, or enemies are always a threat in some areas of the world. In Tunisia, the Berbers went underground to construct houses in artificial craters ten meters deep and connected by a system of tunnels. Eventually discovered by Hollywood, the Tunisian location served as a set for *Star Wars*. It was so incredibly alien looking that it convinced us we were seeing a remote planet.

At the other end of the spectrum, caves have been capitalized upon as stunning places to spend a holiday. A resort in Santorini,

Greece, offers a complex of cave houses with naturally vaulted interiors away from the maddening crowd. Luxurious interiors include a sweeping view over the sea. Tourists can also take day tours to cave houses on the Canary Islands. The tour includes repose on a sunny rock while lunching on goat cheese, potatoes, and garlic sauce. Along the banks of the Loire River in France, families still occupy houses carved into limestone hillsides.

The most notable of cave culture, however, are the cliff dwellings of the Anasazi people at Mesa Verde, near Four Corners, New Mexico. The complex, urbanlike village was carved into rock along canyon walls nearly a thousand years ago. It includes a network of intricate stairways, notched out finger- and footholds on wall faces, multilevel gardens, and elaborate road systems. Multiroom, multistory homes had doors in the sides and roofs for access to living quarters. Openings in the floor led to ceremonial chambers ornamented with great detail. Although the cavernous openings there had been inhabited eight thousand years before Christ, the Anasazi culture thrived for a hundred years about AD 1350. As a fortress, such cliff dwellings are our continent's version of castles; the cliff dwellings remain a significant relic of native peoples.

Chimney Rock Pueblo, at a height of 7,600 feet, is built on the crest of a ridge in precipitous terrain accessed only by walking. The rubble, mud, and mortar construction in southwest Colorado appears as though it was built to coincide with major lunar standstills during the moon rise between Chimney Rock and Companion Rock. Today's American Indian Science and Engineering Society, whose engineer warriors are both builders and thinkers, was organized to preserve past architectural forms like these. They also design new forms of dream homes that facilitate native people's still-viable way of life.

As I contemplate my own dream home, I would not pursue life in, on, or under a rock—unless it was Kokopelli's Cave B&B,

perhaps. From Kokopelli's entrance you can view Southwest sunsets over four states! The waterfall-style shower and flagstone hot tub would no doubt redeem the climb down seventy-five sandstone steps and then a ladder. But proprietors say, "You really have to want to come!"

In the same way, I really have to want to manifest my spiritual dream home before I dare to venture into the caverns of my soul. I'll have to confront my shadow side, that part of me that hides unmentionable needs and fears. That part of me I don't want to talk about, my shadow side, is cold and jagged and too tight fitting. But exploring its terrain, I may discover something I need to build a soul home that is as beautiful, comfortable, and intriguing as Kokopelli's.

The apostle Paul's letters in the New Testament are riddled with insight about our shadow sides. He sums up fairly well the shadow side of human nature in a piece of Scripture we all can relate to: "For the good that I will to do, I do not do; but the evil I will not to do, that I practice. . . . Who will deliver me from this body of death?"[2]

There are many different ways to talk about the shadow side, however. Fairy-tale writer Gordon McDonald touched on it in his work *Phantastes*. The character Anodos suffers a death that is not permanent, then returns to his castle to find he has lost his shadow. He muses, "I have a strange feeling sometimes, that I am a ghost, sent into the world to minister to my fellow-men, or, rather, to repair the wrongs I have already done." Anodos eventually discovers that he is able to love others without needing to be loved in return. "Love gives to him that loveth, power over any soul beloved," writes McDonald.[3]

McDonald is showing that transformation is facilitated by losing our shadow, acknowledging things we would rather conceal. When we bring them into the light of our castle on a hill, our darkest needs and fears are disempowered. We may then love others without needing anything in return.

J. M. Barrie gave us a whimsical visual image of this in *Peter Pan*. Peter discovered that he had lost his shadow at the Darling residence in London. His sidekick, Tinkerbell, went back to find it. The shadow had been rolled up and put in a drawer for safekeeping: "You may be sure Mrs. Darling examined the shadow carefully, but it was quite the ordinary kind,"[4] Barrie writes. Peter returned to get it but couldn't get the shadow to stick to his body until Wendy Darling sewed it in place. After that, Peter and Tink taught the Darling children to fly, and away they went on an adventure with mermaids, pirates, and Indians.

The fantasy, of course, is that we have detachable shadows, says Mick Cope of WizOz.[5] The reality is that they cannot be removed. We must learn to live by disempowering the shadow side—in faith acknowledging our weakness—and then we learn to fly!

In *A Year by the Sea*, author Joan Anderson relates a conversation with a friend who commented around the dinner table, "'At our ages and stages we should be going for the gold of our shadows. Look at the dirt in your life and work with it, instead of avoiding it. You're actually embracing your shadow right now by doing something out of the ordinary pattern, looking at stuff you've probably been afraid to unleash for years.'"[6]

"Our shadows hold the essence of who we are," writes author and therapist Debbie Ford, calling them our most treasured gifts. "It is by embracing all of who we are that we earn the freedom to choose what we do in this world."[7]

In Central Turkey, the Cappadocia valley makes this idea visible in an enchanting material way. The extensive region is formed of odd, conic forms of yellow rock, some topped with off-angle hats up to fifteen meters high. Known as a place of cave dwellers, the valley is home to people who have carved out caves under the cones. When this soft volcanic stone called "tuff" is exposed to air, it hardens. This natural phenomenon allows people to hollow out rooms of any shape or height, since the walls and ceilings do not need supports. In fact, access to the upper rooms was sometimes through a narrow chimney in the middle of the cone. The extensive region is honeycombed with these so-called "fairy chimneys." Some are the retreats of mystics, others the homes of ordinary families. At least 3,500 are rock churches or monasteries dating from the first century. They are free-standing forms that have been decorated with a wealth of ancient sacred drawings. Here the haunting, almost eerily beautiful geography has inspired human habitation and art.[8]

Underground cities burrowed into the tuff of central Turkey were places of refuge where people hid themselves and their families from invaders, raised livestock, and went about their business. One such city extends several kilometers with central squares where streets cross. Large millstonelike rounds of rock were held at strategic locations to be rolled down inclined grooves to seal off the passages. The most recent tunneling occurred when Christians escaped into the earth to avoid Arab invaders in the tenth century. Elaborate systems of ventilation, storage rooms, churches, and connecting passages within the layers—perhaps as many as eighteen—are still being discovered.[9]

It is often the caves of our lives that, like Turkey's fairy chimneys and underground cities, evoke awe, influence the imagination, and inspire us to live inventively, generatively. The writings about such places are as labyrinthine as the catacombs of St. Callixtus, dug in five levels more than twenty meters deep and twelve miles long. These Roman catacombs cover ninety acres along the Appian Way. One epitaph engraved there simply says, "Such Is Our Life," an acceptance that the dark side is part of

163

the light. Reframing the human experience of death as a beautiful passage, another describes the day of a loved one's dying as "The Day She Entered into Light." Talk about learning to fly! From the lower levels, we learn lessons for ministry we couldn't learn anywhere else. Our own cave walls may be God's canvas and parchment.

The entire complex of Roman catacombs winds for six hundred miles outside the walls of that city. It is the cemetery of hundreds of thousands of Christians in the first three centuries, and, experts say, the earliest evidence of a community that changed the course of Western civilization. Expressing its faith while coping with the realities of life, one of which is simply death, the community created an iconographic art form in the catacombs. Most notably Jesus is depicted there as an ordinary man with his hand touching people, offering healing and relationship.[10]

Subterranean places such as the catacombs and the cave churches of Cappadocia have preserved the best of Christian art *because* of their remoteness and protection from sunlight. Should we wonder that the art of our lives—Jesus touching people through us—is being produced and preserved in the darkest times?

In an erosive process, solid rock is being dissolved, so no wonder it hurts. It takes a long time to make a deep cave. What we do with and through and in that cave may change the course of history.

soul PROJECT

Shine Your Light

In Sunday school we sang, "This little light of mine. I'm gonna let it shine. . . ." Then we asked, "Hide it under a bushel?" and shouted with all our might, "No!" Of course not. We believed in ourselves and the light of God within us. But how many times do we fail to let our light shine because we're afraid of being prideful or afraid that we'll fail in some effort or risky, daring endeavor? Mostly, we're just afraid.

Fear is the boldest enemy, the highest obstacle, the meanest hindrance to a life well lived. It will also keep you and me from making our house the best home it can be. Now is the time to answer the old Sunday school question. Are you hiding your light under a bushel basket? And answer a few other questions too:

- What about yourself and/or your home are you dissatisfied with?
- What three things would you most like to change?
- What about yourself and/or your home make you feel most loved and comforted?
- How can you double those qualities through changes to your home?
- What gift for yourself and/or your home would you like to receive today if an anonymous benefactor were to knock on your door? (Something besides money.)
- If you could redecorate your home in any style whatsoever and money was no object, what style would you choose?
- How might you incorporate one thing typifying that style each month this coming year? (Why not create a plan with suggested accessories or steps toward home

improvement even if you think you cannot make it happen?)

- What one single emotion would you like your home to communicate to guests and family?
- What one emotion would you like your friends and family to take away after spending time with you in your home?

Just answering a few questions for yourself will bring answers and insights to light. If you document your answers to these questions in a journal or notebook, so much the better. You will find yourself living the solutions and desires of which you've become conscious.

TWENTY

Crenellated Castles
IN THE AIR

What an interesting life I had. And how I wish I had realized it sooner!

Colette

Once upon a time, not so long ago, I lived for a year or two on the fairy-tale island of Funen, in Denmark, the world's oldest kingdom. On an autumn day, I rode my rickety bicycle down the country road that led from our brick farmhouse through rolling wheat fields. With a gasp—*ahhh!*—behind a stand of beech trees I saw a turreted castle with all the trimmings, as if in miniature, but every bit a royal residence of ages past. A mote filled with water and embroidered with slender nodding reeds and wispy cattails circled the worn structure.

What history might have been written in the forest between our homes? I wondered.

The tight growth of trees looked as if it might be hiding the likes of Robin Hood or Maid Marian. Perhaps there I would find the wild swans, the charmed princes of Hans Christian Andersen's tale. Or maybe the princes' sister, Elisa, might still be wandering in these woods, knitting shirts of nettle she had crushed with bare feet. Tales of castle lore came tumbling across my mind.

What is it about a palace that tugs at our romantic fantasies? Defining one of four females archetypes as that of queen, Carl Jung recognized this as profoundly embedded in our psyche. A castle motif, in which royalty reigns benevolently, looms powerfully over the peasant context of our daily lives. Teresa of Avila drew upon this theme in her sixteenth-century devotional book *The Castle Within*. At the time she wrote it, many castles were crumbling, their proud service as citadel and fortress coming to an end. Yet, to inspire ordinary people, this Spanish mystic tapped into the mystique they held. Describing the journey of the soul toward God, she led readers on an exploration through a castle's many rooms, each different and significant, rendering lessons of virtue, love, and grace.

In actuality the medieval castle was not the posh residence that Teresa of Avila, you, or I may have fancied. Although impressive as symbols of power and wealth, castles were user-*unfriendly* to the minutest detail. Little did they resemble the whitewashed tower with high-flying banners where Cinderella happily-ever-aftered. Castle walls were built to withstand attack, not provide comfortable living space. With no central heat source, interiors stayed damp, and windows were narrow slits through which sunlight—when it did appear—penetrated very little. Blustery winds and rain, however, did invade at every opportunity. Heat and light from fireplace or candles were minimal and dim. Broad stairs going up and down from one level to another required incredible amounts of time and energy. The not-so-private "throne rooms," then, deserve hardly a mention as cold, putrefying experiences. Fortunate was the queen who had a chamber pot under her bed and a chamber maid to empty it each morning.

The purpose of castles, built primarily in the early centuries of the second millennium, was to protect a kingdom from enemies. They were also meant to flaunt the monarch's position. To further establish territory, knights were permitted to build their own castles in surrounding territory. First made of wood and surrounded by a fence called a palisade, the walls were eventually built of stone—taller, broader, and stronger. The castles we romanticize were typified by crenellations along the walls. These offered defensive positions for archers. Round towers at the corners deflected cannonballs from their curved surfaces and prevented undermining of foundations by attackers. But by the fifteenth century, as firearms were developed, castles were no longer impregnable barricades. Most were abandoned for more comfortable abodes.

Hundreds of castles built during the time of the Crusades still survive in Europe and the Middle East. They are trademarks of legend and myth. The stories that grew out of them and their eras of origin still inform our experience. The tale of a young knight named Parzival, written in 1200, is one of these. Parzival is a naive, fatherless child who ends up making too long of a journey in too heavy armor. In search of godliness and chivalry, he embarks on a quest for the Holy Grail, the chalice from which Jesus drank at the Last Supper.

Some years forward, Parzival finds himself in a kingdom where the crops are dying, the waters poisoned, and the king ill. Yet, in the castle, the nobility dances and feasts in merriment. Out of courtesy, Parzival does not question this quizzical paradox. He also realizes too late that it was there he saw the Holy Grail. When years later he sets off to find the castle again, he searches and searches mile after mile, battle after bloody battle, gathering clues to its whereabouts. Finally, its towers loom on the horizon.

Now Parzival discovers the king is on his deathbed. The crops are withered in the field. Dead fish cover the riverbanks and lakes. Still the nobility dance under an enchanted spell with smiles plastered on their faces. Older and wiser, Parzival asks at last, "What's wrong here?" His question—the right question—breaks the enchantment. Immediately the nobility become real. The waters are purified, the crops are renewed, and the king is restored to health. Parzival drinks at last from the holy chalice.[1]

Aren't we, one thousand years later, still seekers of the castle that holds the Holy Grail? Like Parzival, we are on a long journey, looking for its towers. Our quest is to find the chalice from which we may drink deeply of God. The losses along the way are clues given us to identify the daring and honest questions that will break the enchantment of human suffering.

A fortyish woman in my aerobics class recently complained to me of sagging breasts. I thought, *Thank heavens for that*, then mumbled something to her about making peace with time, circumstance, and the losses. I've recognized with a few more years that things like sagging anything are opportunity to break the illusions of the "good life."

Some of us get to practice with superficial losses first—like sagging breasts or the loss of a friend. Others seem to start out in life being forced to deal with the trauma of woundedness, things like childhood abuse, divorce of parents, or loss of a limb or a loved one. I wonder if such young people, forced to fight valiantly onward in spite of despair, are the Parzivals of humankind. They bear the pain of battle and somehow must find the courage to ask the right questions. In that way the enchantment under which the rest of us live, naive and unaware, may be broken. Barely into his teens, Mattie Stepanek, author of *Heartsongs*, is one of these people. He suffers from a rare form of muscular dystrophy and has lost three siblings to the same disease. He admits that not being healed is disappointing. "But you know what?" he asks. "I've had the best time! Because of my attitude."

In the tale of Bluebeard, a woman who has been brought up to avoid asking questions marries the prince. She is given a set of keys to the castle and is invited to use any of the keys except the smallest. Bluebeard is gone on a trip, and the bride's older sisters come to visit and make a game of finding which door is opened by the smallest key.

"Where do you think that door is?" they ask, trying the smallest key in each one.

The question might well have been "What is wrong with this picture?"

It is the right question, for although their younger sister is supposed to become a queen, in fact her murder is being planned. After trying all the other doors, the smallest key is put into the lock of the last. It opens, but to the shocking carnage of many women's corpses—all the corpses of Bluebeard's past wives. The sisters slam the door. The key begins to bleed all over their sister's clothing and body. Her shattered innocence cannot be hidden from Bluebeard when he returns. No longer can she hide behind a smiling façade or censor the pain. It is exactly at that point that she is able to do what she must to escape and rejoin her older sisters.[2]

Who wouldn't want the aura of a romanticized castle to characterize her life? But at what cost? Surely not that of toxic wells beneath an exterior that communicates, "Everything is just fine, thank you."

For years I waited for a fairy godmother to arrive and dress me in crinoline, put wheels under me for the road of life, and put a castle in my future. I was polite, courteous, and dared not ask rude questions. Eventually, life—my metaphorical sisters—pushed me into cold waters, a journey far bloodier than expected. I would earn the forthrightness to ask myself, *What's wrong with this picture?*

I am grateful to be alive at all, and though innocence has been stolen from me, I continually re-create a second innocence. Once upon that time not so very long ago, on the verge of everything or nothing at all, I decided to believe that fairy tales really do come true. I decided I would no longer remain enchanted by doubt and fear. In the crenellated castle of my dreams, I am the brave little princess, the plucky heroine, and the fairy godmother of my own life. I tap into epiphanies by asking sacred questions, and they set me free. There are many rooms yet to be explored, and I have learned to use any key I choose.

soul PROJECT

Celebrate the Beauty of Imperfection

There is nothing more whole than a broken heart," an anonymous Jewish rabbi is often quoted. We miss that truth too often. We fail to see meaning in the flawed things. We are not conscious of the power in an image of brokenness. Putting wildflowers in a favorite vase that is cracked or stained values what has been meaningful in the past. Mending a torn seam carries the value of that piece of clothing into the future.

Our lives are full of flawed objects, so why not appreciate the place they have in our lives and the lessons they have to teach?

A German cream pitcher, a gift from my grandmother, was broken when the wind blew it off its window perch. A string of amber stones broke when it was caught on a screw as I lifted it from my jewelry box. My heart has been broken by someone who didn't value my love. My red jacket, the one I wear daily to fetch the wood that heats my home, has a broken zipper. My favorite CD broke when it fell out of my car and was stepped on. I broke a big jar of freshly made strawberry jam as I was putting it into the refrigerator.

Some of these things required that I cut the losses and throw them away. Others I salvaged and still use because I appreciate their ongoing value or the sentiment attached to them.

Does your home harbor broken things? Confront the facts. Know when to toss the keepsakes and still preserve the memories. Know when to realize there is nothing more beautiful than a particular object that has been scarred by time and use and love. Give yourself permission to make a decision about the broken things in your home and in your life.

- *Save love letters from relationships that, though broken, still brought you gifts of Soul.* (Discard those from the jerks in your life.)
- *Repair objects that were inherited or given by a special person or on a special occasion.* They are symbols of life's beautiful imperfect things: our bodies, our ambitions, our dreams.
- *Replace anything that would cost more in time or money than it is worth to you.*
- *Validate the significance of objects to which your soul responds:* A bird with a broken wing may be buried with ceremony. The dress you wore to that special dance may be made into glamorous pillows for your bed. Your grandfather's worn-out clock may be placed on a shelf as a token of what his presence meant in your life.
- *Declutter spaces by untangling what you want to keep from what has no place of poignancy in your environment.* Throw away the nonkeepers with grace and gusto.
- *Box up (labeled) anything that has some practical or sentimental value.* In one year, if you have not dug it out to use it or have not thought about it at all, let it go.

TWENTY-ONE

The Art of
LIVING INTERIORS

I can't paint. I can't write. I can't sing. But I can decorate and run a house and light it and heat and have it like a living thing.

Elsie de Wolfe

The mysteries always teach us to combine the holy with the profane," theologian Martin Buber said. That same insight is expressed in another way—doctrine without jargon—by decorator Elsie de Wolfe. An attitude toward home interiors like De Wolfe's enhances our sense of the holy to ground our busy, fragmented lives. When we incorporate visual elements in our home that spring from our desire to worship, we express spirituality in the raw stuff of life.

Your décor may be inspired by high-church environments that feature rich color, ornament, and embellishment. Or it may be inspired by minimalist congregations where neutral colors, sheer light from transparent windows, and plain furniture facilitate simplicity. It may be inspired by nature, particularly the celestial realm as filtered through the heritage of Judeo-Christian tradition: stars, sun, clouds.

However you combine the sacred with the ordinary will keep the flame burning on the hearth of your dream home.

"Color is the first thing we respond to when entering a room, the most powerful decorating tool, because it affects how we feel," according to designer Gail Mayhugh.[1]

Marketing analysts claim also that color is a tool of communication. Since color can actually shape mood and biological responses, it greatly affects the sacred possibilities in our homes. Much like scent, memories are attached to different colors; individual color preferences are often based on our own experience of emotions associated with places or events.[2]

In the twenty-first century, consumers seek healing colors—colors that create soulful feelings, even down to the rejuvenating hues chosen for bath towels. For the new millennium, the Color Marketing Group predicted earth tones and shades of water and sky would predominate in response to consumers' interest in spiritual things. At its dawn, true red, the color of religious iconography, was most popular, possibly in connection with the anniversary of Christ's birth celebrated around the globe. Deeper reds, burnt reds, and bluish reds came soon after, symbols of connection to regal heritage as children of God and to the creation. Purples and blues were popular as soothing colors. They make visible transcendence, cleansing, and clarity. The light we love in white brings a tie to purity and emotional comfort. Subtle browns make their way into the earthy palette with names like "biscotti" and "mocha," inspired by the popularity of coffeehouse hot spots—substituting for some the fellowship previous generations found in church.[3]

Artful interiors reflect your saga: your personal history, family tradition, and ethnic culture. The decorating choices you make usually are determined by what is happening in your life and what you want to happen. "A person's home should be like a three-dimensional scrapbook," says art gallery director Greg Guelda.[4] When you allow your interiors to evolve, when you make even subtle changes in your living space as you do in your life, that re-creates what you will experience as well. Questions are pertinent: Where did you travel this year? How were you influenced by the terrain and the customs? Will this be reflected in your home next year? What changes occurred in your family? How did you celebrate differently? What new traditions did you start? What books did you read and classes did you take? What new thoughts and ideas were generated by these? What kinds of objects, colors, and design will reflect this in your rooms? How will all these changes influence how you will live and what you will do differently in your life and family next year?

A glimpse into a couple of pages of my three-dimensional scrapbook reflects recent changes in my life:

- I found that I preferred furniture to be arranged at diagonals. Afterward I read that doing so is an antidote to disharmony collecting in corners. (Does that mean I'm doing the right thing, or that I should work on the disharmony in my home? This has become an interesting question for me to ponder and may lead to more changes.)
- I had a delightfully animated goldfish for years—until he leapt to his death one day. Since then, without conscious connection to the goldfish, I played with the idea of painting my front door red. I read that according to feng shui, the ancient art of "placement," a goldfish or a red door invites prosperity. Wouldn't that be nice?

- Ever since I can remember, my shelves have served as little altars where I place icons like the lava rock from my hike to the top of Black Crater or mosaic pieces picked up along the Apian Way near Caesarea. Recently I learned that rocks and stones are elemental symbols of Saint Patrick's Celtic Christianity.

As an experiment, I write questions for myself and tuck them into vases and pitchers, under candlesticks, and in books: What does my home want? What kind of person is my home inviting me to be? What concrete steps might take me there? What does my sofa want to wear? What messages do the walls want to pass along? If I could do one thing different this year, what would it be?

I will allow myself to live into the answers, educated by a rural existence close to nature, where weathered things mingle with new. Wear and tear is part of the charm. My windows don't want to dress up, for instance. My fireside chair requests contours that hug and feel plush with wear of soft-on-the-skin upholstery. My walls ask for a dash of the theatrical: a colorful hat on the antler rack, a bright painting hung upside down.

My house is filling itself with symbols of where it wants to go—clutter-free, for one thing. It does not want to be overly attached to the past. That would imply fearing the future won't bring anything as meaningful as what has gone before. Sentiment is often just a different kind of materialism that only seems less inane. My home will always be a work in progress.

Some things never change, of course, but very few. Among these, empty space in a room is universally essential. White space, as it is called in graphic design, leaves a place for personal interpretation and for emotional response to be processed. Along with light, empty space can enhance the sacred feel of an interior more efficiently than anything else. It invites something new to happen. But no interior style or any certain look exists in and of itself. There is more going on in your interior than what is visible. Awaken the room to pleasing sounds. A little fountain in a corner can soothe the stress of a city and actually soften body language. A sense of smell does not have to be awakened with artificial scents from sprays or candles—branches of a tree, herbs grown in pots, biscuits in the oven all work to make a house a home. The things you touch, the tactile, add to the home experience too: the texture of the fabrics, your carpets or woods, tiles, plaster, and other surfaces and exteriors.

In décor a fundamentally sensual response is at work with the spiritual. I found myself bringing earthy things into my home: terra-cotta, iron, pebbles smoothed by river water, beach stones pocked by organisms and waves, spice-colored things like the red cinder on the roads where I live. I wouldn't trade anything (anything!)—even convenience—for wood heat and firelight. If I buy jewelry, it is usually garnet and amber. I decorate with these too, hanging necklaces on pretty hooks or heaping bracelets in a crystal dish. Whenever something in a shade of blue was brought into my home, I found myself moving it around, then moving it out. Recognizing this pattern helped me learn more about myself.

I read that some people need to be cooled down, others to be warmed up. I discovered that fire represents creativity while water represents activity and movement. Pinks and reds have long been associated with femininity, and blues with masculinity. Investigating further, I recognized at last that having lived so long in a household of females (including all their female friends coming and going), my home harbors a lot of female energy—possibly an overload. Watching a random *Home and Garden* TV program, I learned that blues and the color black must be used to anchor reds. Now I've planted such anchors in my living spaces: a dark blue throw over the sofa, a carpet incorporating dark blue triangles with burgundies, a blue satin housecoat on the wall in my bedroom.

My goal is to create an artful journal of place and history in my home. That does not mean a "pulled together" décor that communicates a particular style or offers a coherent look. Flaws let in light. Imperfections and all, my home will reflect that which is most meaningful for me, peace and a lively sense of fun. Why not have both? Home is where you live the life you really want, says Jane Alexander, author of *Spirit of the Home*. There are no perfect lives and there are no perfect homes, she explains, concluding that a home is made numinous by the love and feeling we invest in it.[5]

Frank Lloyd Wright believed that architecture is the master art form, and he reinvented it according to his own vision. Designing and building 769 buildings in his lifetime, both monumental and intimate, Wright saw that the space where people live would make the people who inhabit it different. He sometimes stipulated interior design for his homes as well, right down to where each table and chair should be placed.

Wright's view of art was described by historian William Cronon: "An artist . . . transforms nature by looking at nature, passing it through the soul, and in the expression . . . something more natural emerges. Which is as close as we get to God."[6]

Indeed. Our homes and the sacred art of living in them are a link between heaven and earth. Invite God in.

soul PROJECT

Create a Sacred Space

The art of decorating and the art of creating sacred space start with the same elements, according to Mary Groves.[7] As codirector of the Sacred Art of Living Center in Bend, Oregon, Groves is intimately involved with planning the ambience of programs and presentations as well as content. "Both décor and sacred space involve beautiful items," she says. "Both involve the use of color themes, fabrics, live plants, birds, or fish—and design, the manner in which they're put together—to change a room."

After completing an interior decorating course earlier in her life, Groves realized that the only people who could afford her service would be the wealthy. She says that idea turned her off: "I wanted to do this for people who shop at Wal-Mart. I wanted to go into somebody's home and help them rearrange what they've already got."

Working for years with Hospice, Groves realized by visiting people's homes as a volunteer and bereavement coordinator that beyond the way a home is decorated, everyone has altars in their living spaces. "We all display things that are important to us," she says. Groves realized that the element of *significance* is what makes them not just decorations, but sacred objects. "Rather than putting my collection of mementos or trophies on this shelf because I'm proud of them," Groves says, "I recognize it's more than that. These things represent a lot of energy that I've put into life. They stand for who I am. The intention with which I place them make them more than just something to look at. They become an extension of me, an expression of my soul."

Groves now creates altars and sacred spaces for educational

workshop environments—the Art of Spiritual Discernment, the Sacred Art of Dying, and Taize Vespers worship, an interfaith prayer service. "My belief is that all things are sacred," she says. "What we do with them either depletes us or inspires us to live in a better way." Groves's interior settings create a sense of God's presence as well as beautiful backdrops that become centers of spiritual focus.

How might you transform the interior decoration in your home into sacred space? How might you create altars to God through your home?

- *Pay attention to light, arrangement, and symbolism.* An altar can be set up anywhere. It may even be carried with you in a small box. Just a little candle placed with care on a desk can transform practical space to a place of prayer.
- *Altars are made when you carefully arrange photographs of people you love or miss,* items that represent places you've been, objects in which you've invested energy, colors that have a particular significance. These may change the emotive content of a room.

As Groves says, "An altar is nothing more than a place to remember someone or something that is important to you." It is a place to inspire you to live on and to live well.

PART 4

Ode to Everyday
EXTERIORS

TWENTY-TWO

Keep a
BEACON BURNING

We are obsessed with lights. Not random lights, but carefully arranged ones. Perhaps it is our way of hurling the constellations back at the sky.

Diane Ackerman

They say you can't go home again. But can you? Every time I go through a new crisis, I have to find my way home once more: home to myself; home to what really matters; home to people I love; home to people who love me, even new people and unexpected relationships. During the journey, my hope is that when I find my way back home again, someone will have kept the porch light burning.

During eight wacky years as a single mom, my kids both drove me crazy and kept me sane. We went through a lot of lightbulbs during their teenage years, many of them illuminating the driveway and front porch. Traffic in and out was steady, and the deck out front saw a lot of wear. Repeatedly, the crunch of car tires in gravel signaled the girls' arrival back after bedtime. Headlights would stream through my bedroom curtains while they said their good-byes to their main squeeze. Even when rudely awakened, I was always grateful, for the girls were the light of my life.

Sometimes roles reversed and they took their turns waiting up for me. It seemed they seldom remembered to turn on the porch light, however, except when I least appreciated it—arriving home from a date. Kissing good night in the glare of a porch light was not the way I wanted to end a rare romantic evening. I'd come in and they'd act nonchalant, but always with odd little smiles at the corners of their lips.

My identity rests no longer in that of a single mom but in that of a single woman—and that's a profound change. In the transformation, I learned an important lesson: If I don't switch on the porch light for myself before I leave home, I'm going to arrive home in the dark.

The street I live on has no street lamps. Too often I've pulled into my dark driveway and come up dark porch steps to a dark house. I've disappointed myself time after time, forgetting to leave a light burning before I leave. Unless the moon is waxing, I stumble up the steps, fumbling for the front door key. I slide my fingers back and forth across the brass plate to find the key-hole and then turn the key from side to side trying to figure out how—up or down?—to fit it into the lock. I'm not complaining. Being single again has taught me that when I come right down to it, married or not, parent or not, I'm the only person to whom I am 100 percent accountable. I am the only person who will never leave me. I am the only person with whom I will live every day the rest of my life. If I want to come home to a front porch bathed in sweet light, I'd better be my own Thomas Kinkade.

You know Thomas Kinkade, who has trademarked his name as "The Painter of Light" and has created a landslide business with his fine art. He paints soft, diffused light coming from the windows of cottages, cabins, Victorian homes, and other idyllic abodes. The light he brings to the canvas illuminates the landscape and suggests home as a container for life and love. There is something about that kind of warm, glowing scenario that allures. Judging from the sales, it appeals to a huge number of people. How did Kinkade find that magic something? What is our culture missing that gets us to plunk down our hard-earned money to get a nostalgic feeling facilitated by a painting on the wall of our home?

I don't own a Kinkade painting, but I know the mesmerizing settings from honest-to-goodness experience. For years I walked with my father before dawn around the loop of our country subdivision—small houses tucked into half-acre lots in the woods. We met on the corner between our homes at 5:30 a.m., rain or shine, four seasons of the year.

In winter, smoke from chimneys curled under our noses with whiffs of juniper or fir. All was quiet in the neighborhood except when icy snow crunched under our boots. Dim light shone from the windows as people rose to start their day. It reminded Dad of kerosene lanterns, the ones he used throughout his childhood. It set him talking about the good old days, and his longing backward kindled my interest in the history of keepers of the flame.

The tradition began along the Mediterranean shore about 660 BC when a bonfire was built atop a visible point as a guide for ancient mariners to guide their ships to port. Later, in other parts of the world, these were built atop brick towers as beacons for sailors.[1] Eventually the fires were replaced with a single candle whose light was reflected and refracted. Hundreds of candles were necessary to guide ships through a single night. Today's electrified lighthouses produce an intensity of over a million candlepower. Although a Global Positioning System can pinpoint a navigator's position, says Captain Larry Walker, "when a 15-cent component fails, we still hope that someone left a light on for us. Some things never change."[2]

In the parable of the seven virgins, Jesus instructs us to have our lanterns filled with oil before the bridegroom arrives.[3] This gentle rabbi, who saw us as innocent as virgins, wanted us to keep the light and love burning in our own spirit at all times. The lesson has many layers. It is Jesus' admonishment about his second coming, and I also see it as sweet anticipation of calling and the challenge to be what God wants me to be in his kingdom. If I don't keep the light burning on the front porch of my life, what will happen when handsome opportunity—to engage in love or to serve—comes knocking at my front door?

The poignant lyrics of Scottish composer Angus Macleod bring this idea firmly home. In his native Gaelic, he sings, and also in English:

> Last night I had the strangest dream,
> The strangest dream of all.
> I dreamt I saw my grandfather
> Walking in the hall.
> There are things that you don't know about.
> This I can see.
> So keep your porch light burning strong.
> Through eternity.[4]

Jesus boldly proclaimed that we are the light of the world.[5] Why hide our candle under a bushel basket when it is meant to shine before all humankind? I hope to keep a beacon burning to inspire and comfort others. I want to be starlight's silvery luminescence for someone walking through a dark night of the soul. I hope that children will find cozy refuge by the fire that flickers in me. I vow to create for myself a home where light spills both into the windows and out of them.

"Don't try to drive the darkness out," sang the Second Chapter of Acts, one of the first contemporary Christian music groups that formed alongside the Jesus Movement of the 1970s. "You just turn on the light."

How simple is that?

Thomas Edison proved that light is all around us all the time. Our lamps are testament to the fact that we just have to tap into the power source. Edison's hunch that we could harness electricity to improve our quality of life and the result of his tireless experiments generated a tsunami of change for most of the world.

Suddenly, instead of dealing with the complexities of fire fueled by raw materials to illuminate our homes, all we have to do is throw a switch. Humankind no longer has to wait for the sun to dawn in order to go to work. Nor do we have to retire at sundown.

And yet hasn't the ability to access power always been as close as our fingertips?

If you are walking in the darkness right now, the good news is that electromagnetic waves are all around you. On a spiritual level, the light of the world through the kingdom of God is within you. Perhaps you just haven't turned on the switch, adjusted your antennae, or stepped into it. Designed wonderfully complex, every new baby in the world comes equipped with untold possibilities. Just as a female infant is born with more than 40,000 eggs in her reproductive system, the potential to manifest God's glory is already there. By grace, we're created in God's image: brilliant and illumined.

Did the Garden of Eden come equipped with the lightbulb, the radio, and the microwave?

No, but God knew that sooner or later somebody would figure it out, and he left the pleasure of discovery with humankind. As Master Designer, he relies on the quality of his own workmanship the way a professional relies on a machine he engineered to do what it was created to do.

My friend Dan builds the world's fastest single-engine airplane from a kit for private pilots. The process takes a minimum of one year. During that year, Dan tests and retests every component. Someone once asked, "But what happens if the engine fails—there is no second chance?"

Dan didn't miss a beat: "When I build 'em," he said, "it doesn't fail."

I believe that's the way God built us. We are designed with the capacity to fly—if we dare, held in the everlasting arms. He has already given us everything we need to succeed.

A friend confided in me that he was unhappy about his daughter's lifestyle and had done everything he could think of to lead her out of it, including much prayer. I thought of Dan and God and Thomas Edison.

All I could think of to say was, "Just leave the porch light burning—no matter how late it gets." Leave that light on no matter how busy you get, no matter how kids stray or how long they stay away, no matter how often you disappoint yourself, or how often night falls. Keep a beacon burning.

soul PROJECT

Simply Live

The concept of living simply so that others may simply live is not so much a question of dos and don'ts as a conscious lifestyle choice. One must be wise as a serpent and innocent as a dove in making this choice. If you go in search of tips and hints, you'll find experts seeking your dollars in order to put tools and resources into your hands—just more clutter for your bookshelves and less money to give away.

Begin by knowing that uncomplicating your life is an individual process and an intentional one. It is as much a turning away from former attitudes as turning away from things; it's more about *wanting* less than *buying* less—replacing that persistent ache to *have* with a consistent focus on relationships and experiences that bring wisdom.

We can organize our lives around this choice in specific ways. The first step is to shop (whether for basic groceries, furniture, or vacation packages) with this question on your lips: Does this purchase align with my spiritual and practical values?

Next, take this assessment and apply it to what you think you need. Embrace freedom from need. Living with less requires understanding that less is more. Change your mind about material needs. Challenge yourself to feel differently when you make purchases that serve no sacred purpose. Add to your life only what is easy to clean and easy to move and what will not add to your list of things to do.

Also remember that living simply is not about withdrawing from the world but about eliminating the clutter of our culture and the power of the consumer voice in your home. Here are a few of the basics:

Love people, not things.
Give to others for the cause of justice.
Reduce debt.
Eliminate clutter in your home and schedule.
Learn to do things for yourself (repairs and improvements).
Grow and prepare your own food.
Compare prices.
Live from your higher self.
Worship God.

TWENTY-THREE

Beautiful Borders
AND BOUNDARIES

Enlarge the place of your tent,
And let them stretch out the curtains of your dwellings;
Do not spare;
Lengthen your cords,
And strengthen your stakes.
For you shall expand to the right and to the left.

Isaiah 54:2–3

Do fences make good neighbors? Quoting his neighbor, Robert Frost said so but didn't believe it himself. I side with Frost. Living on the West Coast and in the less-inhabited wilds of our country, I have relished open spaces—what there are of them between thick stands of tall pines. In my humble housing development, fences were open rail and built only if necessary as corrals for horses. Rail fences have an aura of Clint Eastwood about them and provide an open line of vision through to aspen trees or fields of grass. An occasional dog passes through, herds of deer jump over them, or a wandering schoolkid ducks under. Rail fences reveal the layers of natural life.

The house next door to me changed hands last year. The new owner built a tall plank fence between my property and his. It is an opaque fence, like a scar along our property line, an emblem of neighborly isolation.

I think back to childhood—the years my family lived in a bungalow in Kansas. There were no fences between homes in those days. Then, in rural California, no fences were necessary around our plum orchard or any of the other local ranches. I walked straight through an orange grove to the chicken ranch to buy eggs from the Dutch family "next door." In those days, barriers between neighbors didn't seem necessary. I thought the world would always be like that.

A population boom has changed everything, including a shift from small farming to big farming. Jobs are in the cities. The housing trend has shifted from small bungalows to medium-sized ranch-style homes to huge multilevel houses on tiny lots.

This year my oldest daughter and her family purchased a prim two-story house in an urban area. On three sides, neighbors are just an arm's reach away. From any window, a bevy of plank fences creates odd lines in each direction as far as the eye can see. When I voiced my disdain (as nicely as possible), my son-in-law told me with genuine kindness and sincerity that they were thrilled anyway just to have a yard where they can plant a tree, create flower beds, build a deck, and place a sandbox for their toddler.

Their situation is the challenge nowadays—to fashion borders around your house that create a feeling of expansion in constricted areas. Landscape designers will eagerly show you how to accomplish this by creating various levels of earth in a small space. The illusion makes you feel you're in the middle of more space than you actually have. Other illusions are used today too, such as camouflaging fences and making spaces for gathering that draw us outside—an escape from the workaday world; and creating *living* rooms, that is, rooms that are actually alive and designed with organic elements such as plants and vines, trainable trees such as willows, fruit trees such as apple, and floors of earthen brick, flagstone, or wood.[1]

Yet aren't the boundaries of our spaces what define the delight quotient of our dwelling? Intent upon living mindfully, we offer attention to our residence as a place that serves the soul. Privacy, being a universal need—especially in overpopulated areas—means that borders to our homes are a big factor for home owners.

I have studied the small suburban yards in my daughter Tirza's neighborhood. The creative ways people make a positive statement astound me. Small trees and shrubs cluster in pots on porches and balconies. Flowerbed borders blossom with tiny marigold rows or lush rhododendrons. Old-fashioned white picket fences surround yards, with lattice arbors serving as thresholds. Doors are decorated with seasonal wreaths and a palette of zesty colors. Water features outdo each other in swish, spurt, and sprinkle—spectacles of cascading moisture. Almost every entranceway has a stone sculpture hidden among foliage or sitting on the stoop, and I've wondered if these were gifts or chosen by the home owners to reflect their personalities. Gnomes with various expressions are replacing fairies. Even garden angels have begun to seem dated. Bunnies and cat sculptures still prevail.

"The objects with which we surround ourselves in that most familiar and stable environment—the home—are particularly salient expressions of self," writes Clare Cooper Marcus, a landscape architect and professor of architecture at the University of California at Berkeley. "The more we are able to touch those objects, the more we gain reassurance of their reality, a reassurance and a level of relating not gained from sight alone. At some unconscious level, we all know this."[2]

I wonder about this in light of the prophet Isaiah's words, "Enlarge the place of your tent, stretch your tent curtains wide, do not hold back; lengthen your cords, strengthen your stakes."[3] Maybe the boundaries we create around our homes and the stories we reenact through them are a postmodern way to lengthen our cords.

After my divorce I took the words of Isaiah to heart. Since I fought hard to hang on to our home, I wanted to validate the fact that I and the girls stayed put. I wanted to redefine the borders in my own way. There was so much I wanted to do but couldn't afford! I did what I could, and doing what I could was saturated with fulfillment. I painted our front door a new color and hung a new porch light. Each summer I extended the lawn farther than the previous year by watering it then mowing it with extended boundaries. I hauled in sod to sculpt the edges and planted a new tree in commemoration of my new life.

In the process I realized that on any particular day we can increase the significance of the land we do possess when we individualize our space—change it and make it suit our sensibilities. We act out a propensity to nurture living things. We love what we have been given. Gardening can be one way to mark our territory with sacred meaning, but there are other ways, like the ones I tried, too.

In the end, when we cannot enlarge our space, we enlarge the way we think about it and feel about it. So it was for me. After enlarging the borders of my lawn, I wanted to enlarge the borders of my life. I learned to dance, a huge accomplishment since I'd never been allowed to dance when I was growing up. Dancing took all kinds of expressions and brought a great deal of joy. Once, out with a girlfriend at a favorite spot, my ex-husband walked in with a date and was seated at the table directly behind me. Instead of becoming disgruntled about that, I practiced enlarging my borders by choosing to fight hurt and woundedness. Instead, I chose to focus on life, the dance, and the moment. Choosing laughter and hope, I had more fun that night. Instead of looking back, I was looking ahead and never noticed when my ex left the place. Not only did I get the last dance; I got the last laugh.

What about you? Is your life hemmed in by gawky fences? Is your mental energy drained by enclosures meant to keep others out but that serve to imprison you? Are your horizons cut off by a length of ugly planks? Look in new ways at the resources you do have. Use them to your advantage. I was nonplussed when I heard about a fellow making millions of dollars selling Oregon pinecones on the Internet. My yard and common ground is littered with pinecones, so why didn't I think of that? The ridiculousness of the idea got my wheels to whirring. Why not look at everything in my own "backyard" as priceless material for leading the good life?

There are lots of metaphorical ways to enlarge the borders and boundaries of your space, whether it be your life or your home. You don't even have to live in a traditional house on a defined lot to practice this powerful act. No matter what your emotional state and no matter what your individual troubles, there are times when the authentic solution is simply that: to enlarge your borders. Do something you've never done before: Dream big. Move on. Use what's in your own backyard.

Most people in the world's largest cities live in apartments—door to door, wall to wall, living on top of or underneath other people's living space. Most people on earth live in close vicinity to each other. Borders may consist of an iron railing around a tiny balcony or simply a pair of window boxes. Enlarging borders in some cases means cultivating herb gardens in those window boxes or bringing in a potted tree for the balcony. Some people rent a few square meters in a summer garden, a postage stamp–size plot of land on the outskirts of a city or on an empty lot between high-rises downtown. Here an urban dweller can grow a bunch of flowers for the table or a few vegetables for dinner. It isn't the product that is important but the fulfillment of puttering outside in the soil, a defining element of creating borders.

There is a time to maintain borders, a time to enlarge them, and a time to minimize them as well. Humankind is designed, after all, for community and connection. For a time my family and I lived in a compact one-story row house where all the fences were short, only three feet high. That meant casual access to neighbors with the friendly exchange of recipes, news, and kids. Community happened quite naturally. A neighbor child, strawberry-haired Henrietta, lived several houses away but often played at our house. I'll never forget the night she showed up sleepwalking at our door in the middle of the night and started carrying on a dreamlike conversation. I donned robe and slippers and led her safely home again. The experience bonded us with her parents in a way that cannot happen in this day and age of carefully guarded privacy—and tall plank fences.

Would you know your neighbors if you met them in town? (I have to admit, I wouldn't recognize some of mine.) Suburbanites come home each evening and drive through garage doors powered with a remote. In that way no one has to know what we look like—and, hideously enough, we are getting used to it. We've come a long way from the milkman at the door, picket fences you could see through and talk over, and clotheslines where people enjoyed hanging out with one another while hanging out the clothes. Perhaps our task today is to make workable and beautiful landscapes that welcome others into our territory—physical, emotional, and spiritual.

Friends I met overseas who were embassy diplomats taught me the importance of becoming acquainted quickly with neighbors. "We aren't in one place very long," they told me.

In the age of transience, this is true for all of us. My neighbors sometimes move in and out before I've had a chance to see what they look like. My mission includes a promise to meet, mingle, and make a garden for the people who pass through my life. When they, or I, move on—to another place or another dream—the good things will remain behind.

No matter what the fences of my life look like, I hope always to keep a gate open.

soul PROJECT

Comfort in Many Colors

I have to own up to it. Home isn't necessarily, or even usually, signified by sweet memories and nurturing connections. Home comes with many faces. Sometimes home is where the hurt is. Sometimes home is the place where years of growing up take their toll rather than give you wings.

My family home on Wedgemere Road is where I came of age, plucking a ritual blossom from its honeysuckle vine out front when leaving for school each day, tasting the tender droplets on my tongue. It was the home where I spent the years of my adolescence, an often gray period of fluctuating hormones, nightly black-and-white images of the Vietnam War, and growing disillusionment with government, as well as my own changing ideals to fit grown-up realities. Remembering the simple battleship-gray house awakens little nostalgia. Within the walls of that home, many of my viewpoints began to diverge from those of my parents. For good or bad, it was there that I began to seek my own design for living—clumsy and bumbling, but nevertheless taking ownership for my personal experience in the world.

Home, after all, is the place we're meant to outgrow. It is where, if we're healthy, we leave the people through whom we have arrived on this earth—those who are meant to inspire us to find our own way. If home were always and forever sweet and nurturing, who would ever want to leave?

Find how comfort and home are colored for you:

- Ask, "When has my home not been a comfortable place to be?"
- Think of how comfort speaks many languages: the acceptance of differences, ownership of what was, knowledge that what's happened in a particular place does not have to impact what may be happening now (or, for that matter, the future), and the reframing of how love looks.
- Note in your journal or on a piece of paper how home, family, and love express themselves in a myriad of different colors. Try to identify some of those colors. Name what they mean to you.

TWENTY-FOUR

Gear Up
FOR GARAGES

Buddy Holly launched his band in one. The Apple Computer was invented in another. Even Walt Disney holed up in the concrete confines of one to start his animation studio. When Americans want to expand their minds or living areas, most of them turn to the same place: the garage.

Jodi Mailander Farrell

What do you make of a home that does not have a garage? My house maintains this distinction. There is no dwelling place for my Japanese version of the national icon spawned by creative tinkerer Henry Ford. There is no place for the cat box, a freezer, or things accumulated for a summer tag sale. No storage for empty Gateway computer boxes, pickling jars, rakes and shovels, winter tires, or the delightfully useless lamp I got at someone else's tag sale. No roof to protect me from rain so I can paint that old bookshelf. No space to save

201

my daughters' childhood souvenirs. No place, of course, for all the changes that life brings: little bikes, then big ones, a revolving variety of hobbies, clothes in all sizes waiting for thrift-store pickup, or the seasonal decorations that proliferate each year.

My neighbor, a real estate agent, tells me that my lack of a garage will be a big deficit should I decide to rent or sell my house. I study all the other houses up and down the street. Sure enough, mine is the only one without a big blank door staring back. Quite plainly, my home does not live up to the American dream. It does not communicate the spirit of American affluence and enterprise to passersby, for if anything in the early part of the twenty-first century, the United States is known and imaged by its automobiles; highways; drive-thru restaurants, banks, pharmacies, dry cleaners, and other drive-thru businesses; and—most significantly—multicar garages.

Let today's media tell that story. For starters, garage gurus have their own magazine, *Garage Trader*; and in the twenty-first century, the garage even got its own coffee-table book.

"It's about time," says author Kira Obolensky, who notes that in 2001, 17 percent of newly constructed homes included a garage for no less than three vehicles. Obolensky covers just about every square inch of ground that has anything to do with the topic of garages and does so beautifully. In fact, I'd give the world to live in any one of the garages photographed exquisitely in her book, which, notably, is subtitled *Reinventing the Place We Park*.[1]

About the time Obolensky's book was released, the cable channel HGTV (House and Garden Television) featured a restored 1896 firehouse garage that was home to the family car (an antique ambulance), a neon-sign collection, and a full-size diner turned playhouse. Another feature showcased a garage with a thirty-five-foot cathedral ceiling and *kiva* fireplace surrounded by overstuffed chairs—all of which were the backdrop for a large collection of racing and rally cars. If anything, the designers of these places deserve a hurrah for imaginatively conceiving luscious variations on the otherwise boring practice of consumerism.

On the Internet, at Toy Island, you can buy a Fisher Price Big Action Garage for small suburbanites; elsewhere you can dig up full-scale accessories for your own garage—a recycling center, pet station, and GARAGE GURU T-shirt for tool worshipers. Surf a little more and you'll find that comedian Phyllis Diller even has her own video on how to hold a garage sale.

So the garage may be a symbol of the American lifestyle, even the American dream, but do we really think of it that way?

Although the word *garage* comes to us from the French, we make no flourishes of the tongue when we pronounce its two luscious syllables—and there is no stylish charm about the concept in our own culture. I have a hunch, though, that even the dullest structure is filled with potential for the mind's reverie back in time.

I have already shared about the fear I associate with one garage from my childhood. The two paw prints just inside the door of the garage terrified my three-year-old self. (Of course, I was afraid of pixies in the curtains and cows in the closet too.)

On the other hand, our Escondido, California, garage was sheer bliss. It served as a roadside fruit stand, a summertime mom-and-pop venture that cost more to carry off than it netted in profit. Set up with stacks of wooden fruit crates and a contraption to hand-sort plums by size, the garage was a container for the sweet aroma of ripe plums picked daily. For a ten-year-old in tattered shorts and stained shirt, standing on the sun-warmed cement slab of the garage floor was paradise. Juicy Santa Rosa plums, rosy and golden, sold quickly or were made into jams, jellies, and compote. Boxes of tiny, underdeveloped plums went to the Smuckers factory in L.A., a two-hour drive in a jalopy truck. Customers came and went from our garage on weekends,

203

enthusiastic about the quality of our fruit. Here the entrepreneurial spirit played out in a context of the five senses and left me a believer in hard work united with adventure.

Eventually my family moved to a home in the suburbs where my parents remodeled the garage for my grandmother. It came to be permeated with the scent of her perfume and was cluttered with things elegant and otherworldly: delicate scarves, various sets of gloves, and her trademark lace collars. For a prominent doctor's wife who had raised a large family in a stately two-story home near the Harry Truman residence, what must she have felt to wind down her life in a garage? A photograph of her beloved stone home surrounded by garden and cherry trees in Independence, Missouri, hung on the wall. I don't remember that she ever complained. Grandma Daisy was enough of a lady to convince me that even in a garage, grace happens.

What memories and lessons were my own children denied by not having a garage attached to our house? Certainly we have our own memories that grew from the deprivation—like getting tough here on the high desert. A garage is not considered a luxury where fluctuating temperatures and unpredictable weather patterns mean a car gets exposed to traumatizing shifts—and so do we. A garage is a necessity that we didn't have. I've helped the girls jump-start dead batteries on rainy mornings, watching them headstrong and primed for the worst like Xena, warrior princess. There is something essentially purifying about being exposed to the elements and learning to work with them, not against them, unprotected and unpampered. Some primeval instinct settles in; it is innately and deeply satisfying to know you can do what you don't want to do, to jump into the fray and rescue yourself. I'm kind of glad we didn't have a garage.

But snowy winter mornings do more than send a chill down the spine when you don't have a garage. Getting to school (never canceled for inclement weather) meant shoveling a path across our front deck, down the steps, and across the yard to the driveway. The girls eventually caught on that snowfall meant getting out of bed fifteen minutes earlier. After coffee and showers, it wasn't unusual to see one of them in slippers and pajamas wielding the wide flat snow shovel with dogged determination. Then she would jump in the car, turn on the ignition, and screw up the heat full blast. With the long-armed scraper, two inches of powder swiped easily off the windshield to filter down her sleeves. Ice under the snow wasn't so forgiving, but the elbow grease painted roses on my daughters' cheeks.

The American garage may be a dubious national trademark, a temple to a pagan god, creating a sea of sameness along the streetscapes of suburbia. But here's betting most of us have our earliest memories located somewhere in its space. Somehow that makes it sacred.

See what I mean and ask yourself: Do I remember hanging out here with Dad, tinkering at his workbench, or helping Mom with the laundry when washer-dryer sets stood in the garage instead of in their very own room? What family reunion suppers or "dinner theaters" on card tables were held here? Who raised puppies here? When did I hide here from an angry sibling or put together a school project here or teach someone younger how to ride a trike within this hallowed space?

Someday when you're old and feeble and can't remember what you had for breakfast that morning, you'll still remember finding kittens when you were only six, born behind boxes in the garage. Such garage stories are rich and ready on the mind.

Of course, such stories may actually be tales of terror, abuse, and bewilderment. These are no less sacred. The important thing, for good or ill, is that a garage tale is marked by discovery or fear and pain or both.

Because most of us get around in cars, the garage marks the territory of our experience. Even when marred by dark memories, we acknowledge that a garage can be holy ground. For better or worse, filled with a brand-new car, a family standby, a beater, a grease monkey's dream, or no vehicle at all, garages will remain an epicenter in our lives.

soul PROJECT

A Question of Style

Your home is a place to explore your style fantasies and can be a canvas on which to paint your hope. After all, you do have plans for the place you live, right? Unleash your creativity and start filling that canvas—make a master list for those plans. Identify the alternatives and the different looks you would like to achieve— maybe even give your collections of precious things a facelift or visibility for the first time. Use the following questions to help you get what you want from a remodel, redecoration, or reinvention of your home style.

- *What is my vision for my home?* What is it I want to achieve within these walls?
- *What is the saving grace of my home?* What would I most want to change?
- *How would I define the style I want?* Chic simple? Ornate Victorian? Southern swank?
- *How best can this be communicated in specific ways:* With color? By objects? By furnishings?
- *What design ideas inspire me most?* How might I adapt these to my home? What will be most challenging in that process?

- *How can I build details of my own sense of style into the big picture?* Which details will I focus on? What don't I want? (This can be as helpful in defining a style as descriptions of that style.)
- *How does my preferred home style fit my lifestyle?*
- *What is at the heart of my home style?* How might I enhance that to bring a sense of the sacred into my home?

TWENTY-FIVE

Porch Swingers and
OTHER PLUCKY PEOPLE

Just think, that we can claim a slice of the sun.

Louis Kahn

The porch—that old-fashioned idea from the good old days—has been reborn. For most Americans, it is a remnant of the time when, as the country song goes, families really bowed their heads to pray and daddies really never went away.[1] The consensus is in: People want the porch back. They want it back not just for architectural charm but for the values it represents.

The porch is the place people roosted before TV interrupted their lives. Summer evenings on a creaky porch swing with both my parents was entertainment that has been lost to succeeding generations. Mother, feet wedged against the railing, waved to the occasional neighbor passing by or worried aloud about Mrs.

Unroe next door. Twilight fell like a blanket on our shoulders. Daddy sang "Somewhere Out in the West" in his wobbly voice. My sister and I chased fireflies, tucking them into peanut-butter jars with holes in the lids. I sometimes extracted the glow lamp from their midsection and placed it on my finger like a diamond. The fragrance of summer air smelled of sweet peas. Ample, unhurried time meant my fill of lap sitting, arms wrapped in arms.

The front porch is where I learned what it felt like to be family. But in the latter twentieth century, the picture became a cliché stereotype, languishing along with hopscotch and jacks. When urban renewal became suburbs, and suburbs became hypersuburbs, something went desperately wrong. The rise of the gated community along class and economic lines fostered division, disconnection, and alienation. In castlelike McMansions common spaces and porches were nearly nonexistent. Sidewalks too were excluded in favor of golf-course-type lawns extending to the street.

Today, however, innovative builders are bringing back the porch. In a surprising reversal of attitude, many families are now demanding a place to hang a bench swing and set a worn wicker rocker—if they're lucky enough to find one.

The lives of children in retro communities, even with their new Craftsman-style affluence, are no more idyllic than those of children in the 1950s. As kids grow up, family time seems to become rare at any economic level. But a short browse on the Internet reveals the same longing articulated over and over again. The words in numerous essays and sermons and on bulletin boards and personal websites confirm what people want: to rebuild a sense of community. The conversation expresses a kind of universal hunger for symbols that facilitate belonging. Since we function in so many isolated spheres, again and again we are saying that we want public greens, sidewalks, and front porches.

209

In fact, one citizen prophet appeals for every building and house to have a "gift" to the street: a porch that invites interaction. Porches are the intermediary element between the privacy we know inside our homes and the public face of the world rushing by. Experts say such spaces seem the most appropriate places to play out essential social rituals.

Speaking of social rituals, one Web user says she grew up in a Sicilian neighborhood where "women yelled at each other across porches." Another notes that our national folk music was born on front porches in small rural towns—and that folk music became the way we talked to each other, commiserated, encouraged each other, and addressed our commonalities.

During a time when members of extended families lived together, porches contained the overflow of life. Grandparents and grandkids hung out together on back porches shelling peas, snapping beans, and swapping stories. This is perhaps best explained in the words of Canadian musician and composer Michael Jones, who has said the changes in our lives come more through story than ideas. The exchange on porches was much like primitive humankind around the fire—one person passing along to others tradition, tribal history, family legacy, and personal insight and wisdom. A circular gathering place was the impetus for dialogue. In its embrace, something happened through us, not just between us.[2]

As a culture, perhaps we have lost the art of storytelling and now, suffering the pain of its absence, are looking to get it back. Where else but on the front porch once again?

In lieu of front porches in the 1990s, many Americans turned to chat rooms to fulfill the need for human fellowship. Many found there a place to practice the old-fashioned art of conversation. Perhaps chat sites reinvented dialogue and storytelling for a new generation, showing that the need is great. But it takes the slow rocking of ideas and stories to communicate in an authentic way. Perhaps resourceful people on the Web will find a way to fulfill their need and then back it up with human presence. Imagine chat rooms as a back door leading to the front porch.

In southern states, porches are known as verandas. I've always dreamed of sipping a mint julep on one of these, or under a white-pillared colonnade with sweet magnolias dropping petals at my feet. Porch life seems to thrive where life is slower. Or does life slow down where porch life thrives?

In fast-paced Southern California, a real front porch is as rare as neighborliness. Although nearly every house has a patio or open courtyard to the rear, these do not reflect the community lifestyle of the Mexican culture from which they are adapted. In Mexico as in Spain, piazzas open to the front are places where villagers socialize and the party happens just because someone drops by.

In any state one may find swooning porches, sagging porches, or sleeping porches. They may be a wraparound style, screened in, covered, or open to the sky. However they're made, their primary purpose is to offer a vantage point from which to observe, muse, welcome others, and engage in the shelter that is human conversation.

My parents' family gatherings on Sunday after church always happened on the cement porch stoop. Aunts lay dish after dish potluck style there. Uncles started hand cranking the vanilla ice cream. I always liked sitting on the lid of the ice-cream freezer, a thick towel serving as a seat, to steady the cold metal container nestled in the tubs of ice. My cousins took turns with the wooden handle while Grandma busied herself setting ironstone bowls and silver-plated cutlery, fetching more rock salt for the ice, and fretting that the little kids might get hurt on the merry-go-round Grandpa had made.

Though the midwestern, plain-and-simple style didn't touch the gypsy soul that lay shrouded within me—it was here, from the front porch, that I was given a taste of life connected to the land, the ever-present wind, and the changing patterns of clouds above prairie.

How often do you see people along your suburban street sitting in stylish retro chairs drinking iced tea on a front porch?

My friend Brenda moved from our rural community back to an affluent neighborhood where house after house is lit up by the eerie glow from wall-size TV screens. She tells me she misses evenings where neighbors walk together, children come out to play, and people are more interested in what kind of music you like than what kind of car you drive.

Just around the corner from me, my dad sits on his front deck (Northwest jargon for "porch") in his aluminum camp chair. He is there, he says, "to watch the parade go by." The parade includes kids riding every size bike imaginable, dogs running at their sides; joggers mingling with Rollerbladers, and walkers strolling around the curve past the house—always with a wave.

Dad hasn't forgotten how to sing, either. These days he's more likely to launch into his own nostalgic version of "Kansas Land." Five children live across the street from him, and one evening the oldest yelled, "Mitter 'mith! Mitter 'mith! We don't care if you sing!" Then the boy added with the same determined but courteous tone, "But we don't want you to." My father laughingly tells the story as often as people will listen. Porches, it seems, not only give us places to tell stories but stories to tell as well.

Perhaps not many of us have a literal front porch, yet don't we all sense some kind of yearning for one? Front-porch experience is a way of being reborn by being present with yourself or someone else. My granddaughter clamors onto my lap, puts her chubby dimpled hands in my hair, and looks curiously at me with huge moonlit eyes. I want to move slowly and giggle loudly and hold her every minute I can. She carries within her this hankering for front-porch time as the day creeps to its close. She knows the front porch is all about letting go of things: the day's business, emotional burdens, unresolved family issues. It's about saying nothing, saying everything.

"Oh, look at all the beautiful flowers." That's what my mom's elderly father said just before he passed away on his Missouri front porch. Was he speaking of my grandmother's garden or of far more beautiful flowers that no one else could see?

When I pass away, I would like it to be like my grandfather, surrounded by beautiful flowers of my life—Tirza, Leyah, Lissa, and Mira—and I hope it will be on my own front porch.

soul PROJECT

Swing into Spring

Cleaning is not my favorite home topic, yet if we see it as an art, there is no telling where it will take us. I like to start with a plan so I don't run into "never-ending syndrome." If we clean randomly, we'll keep seeing dirt and damage in layer after layer and become discouraged before we finish the entryway! Let's walk through every room first to survey every nook and cranny, then do the following:

- *Make three lists:* (1) deep cleaning (window washing or decluttering closets), (2) routine maintenance (clearing cobwebs or polishing doorknobs), and (3) freshening up (dusting and organizing tabletops).

- *Jot down what you need—cleaning supplies and tools or reorganization products.*
- *Create a schedule and timetable to complete your entire house.* One week? Six weeks? Three months? A year? Using a separate calendar just for cleaning, write a particular task or tasks on each day of your calendar that is available to the project.
- *Before starting, buy yourself a gift certificate for lunch at your favorite restaurant and put it away in a safe place.* (Or splurge on one item for your home, wrap it up, and save it as a reward for the end of the spring cleaning project.)
- *Start with a nourishing snack or meal, dress comfortably, tie your hair out of your face, and don a pair of lightweight gloves.* Beginning with your front door or at the heart of your home and working clockwise, declutter the first room along with its cupboards, drawers, and closets.
- *Open all the windows in the room where you are cleaning.* Start at the ceiling and clean downward, sweeping away cobwebs; wiping down walls, doors, cupboards, and countertops; washing windows; and finishing with the baseboards and floor.
- *Celebrate the completion of each room with a favorite beverage or snack.* Give yourself a hug and a pat on the back!
- *Reward yourself when your spring cleaning project is complete.* Get dressed up, grab your lunch certificate, and head on out for fun.

TWENTY-SIX

Landscape
LOVE SONGS

I have bought a house near Lake Harriet, a kind of bum old house but I could afford it. . . . It has a yard two hundred feet deep and full of weeds, golden rod, apple trees, a monstrous oak, thickets. Many people say, "Oh, I don't like so much yard—all that hard work!" But that is the very thing I like about it: plenty of hard work. One gets so strong and lively then.

Brenda Ueland

What makes one house or another appeal to us? The architecture? The details? The location? "I finally came to the conclusion that it is always about the landscaping," my friend Jane Green told me. That summer I never saw Jane without garden gloves and straw hat, working the soil around her cottage that sits on its now-pampered lot across from the local park. What resulted was a whimsical mixture of wild country and styled English garden. Botanical surprises are

215

tucked into the landscape, including all sorts of teapots topping every post in the picket fence—the sort of stuff that turns *ho-hum* into *wow!*

Another of my friends who is a home enthusiast, Launa Herrmann, lives in a Spanish U-shaped adobe house atop an inland California foothill. Red tile roof, terra-cotta courtyard, and semiarid foliage create an exotic aura. But to the rear, adjacent to the pen pasturing Sigmund the Goat, Launa has created a blossoming utopia. A fenced rose garden, replete with meandering brick pathway, unusual bird feeders and houses, and a labyrinth of colorful flowers, accentuates the contrast in landscape. Her philosophy is based on an old English proverb: "Tickle it with a hoe, and it will laugh into a harvest."[1]

Jane and Launa are part of a flourishing trend of home owners indulging their personal whimsies by using them to create a private outdoor paradise.

Let's face it, though, many of us don't have a place, or at least time, to garden. I can barely keep my lawn watered and mowed, let alone plan, plant, and putter in a garden. Today my front lawn, dry and yellow from the frost, is covered with red pine needles and stubs of branches broken by gray squirrels. Does this send a message to my neighbors that I have no neighborhood pride?

Landscape has long been a canvas for one's philosophy and social status. Surely it also intersects with our spiritual "inscape." The natural world functions within and without; our true terrain is where our sense of place finds resonance with our personal story.

Artful attention and arrangement on the grounds of your home, the balcony of your apartment, or the window box outside your rented room can make your space a mini Eden. You may go for the opulent, the exotic, and the tamed, or you may follow a wiser path to paradise. Using plants appropriate for your climate, you may go low maintenance. But that needn't mean boring or plain. When you imitate the natural landscape on your grounds, you're going for the greater aesthetic.

Celts of the fifth century brought their love of nature and their awareness of the sacred into Christianity when they converted, says Bob Abernethy. They were fierce warriors who lived simple lives and valued the hushed, brooding landscape.[2]

Taking this one step further, John O'Donohue, author of *Anam Cara: Spiritual Wisdom from the Celtic World*, says, "The landscape has a huge influence on shaping the rhythm of mind and perception. Celtic spirituality had a recognition of nature as the theatre of divine presence . . . [it was] where divine presence articulated its imagination."[3]

In landscape, and in shaping the landscape of our homes or our lives, we have opportunity to express ourselves as made in God's image, to articulate our imagination. There seems to be no limit to the gardens we may create: container gardens, rock gardens, kitchen gardens, children's fairy gardens, shade gardens, organic gardens, and so on. Whatever we call it, a well-defined landscape can feed the soul as surely as it can add curb appeal—and, my Realtor tells me, 15 percent to the selling price of a home.

I have to admit, my landscape is not well defined but definitely what experts call "low-envy." I wish I could have tall stalks of hollyhocks frolicking alongside fences, aroma-rich sweet peas, and stately sunflowers nodding in the breeze. Instead, a scraggly juniper tree bears tiny pale blue berries in the fall. Miniature fir trees sit primly in terra-cotta-turned-white pots. The trees are disheveled odd shapes. My backyard blueprint does not involve innovative ideas or exquisitely detailed plans. Visual accents of the artificial kind are not my cup of tea. I am shaping a context for a personal experience in the wild, adopting Thoreau's philosophy, for I also believe that "in wildness is the preservation of the world,"[4] or at least the preservation of my particular soul.

So, yes, "natural" reigns in my yard; I've given myself permission to be free-form and messy. The landscape's rocky, volcanic soil is an extension of the lava beds just ten miles away. It doesn't hold moisture well, but the muted desert colors—tan, sage, and mossy brown—have their own kind of glamour for those who have eyes to see. Though I miss the varied elegant greens of a wetter climate, life abounds anyway under crystal-starred nights, the clean rush of myriad rivers, and the red porous earth.

I take landscape tips from my ninety-three-year-old neighbor who has weathered many days here and come up thriving. Marguerite's yard includes plants with names like "sweep the sky," which are lush with yellow blossoms in June. Her "tiny rubies" ground cover, when in full bloom, looks like drops of sparkling blood.

Ms. M. has spent years arranging flagstone in straight up and down patterns, like canyon walls, creating a rugged effect that imitates Native American geography on the reservation just east. She has hauled down mountain driftwood, carved by eons of wind and parched white as if by the ocean, from hikes along local glaciers. The enigmatic shape of her landscape accentuates the high-desert, high-flying appeal of her home.

I have come to appreciate what desert landscape teaches: Hang on. Hold out. Endure. What does survive is precious. Beauty is in the discernment of the delicate scents in different kinds of sage or the mute tones of trees where wildlife hides. Lack of moisture in the sky creates clarity just like lack of distractions creates transparency of soul. I think of Moses, prince of Egypt, living forty years in the desert, growing tough and sinewy herding animals from place to place. Might he have wondered if he'd missed his life's calling because of mistakes made in his youth? We only know that when one day he saw the burning bush and heard the voice of God, he was an old man shaped by the wilderness. God found him where he was and called it holy ground.

Indeed, landscape tells a story.

What stories will your landscape tell? They are not all sweet or pretty, roses and lavender. I planted a hawthorn tree in front of my house to celebrate my new life as a single woman. Not long afterward it died. The Chinese plum tree planted by my ex thrived, of course, even though it was never watered. I like this story that until now only my landscape knew. The landscapes of our lives are full of mysterious paradox, perplexing puzzles, and peculiar people. They remind us not to take ourselves too seriously. They teach us to pause just to wonder. The landscape is what it is. Our story evolves from moving through it.

"Gardens slow things down," writes Dominique Browning. She knows they help us tell our stories. "I want simply to teach my children to see the roses," she adds. "One day they will know enough to stop and smell them, too."[5]

Do you live in a manicured neighborhood or along a rambling country road? Are you blessed with lush and fertile soil, or do you have to haul it in? What are your favorite flowers? Colors? Scents? Everyone would like profuse blossoms, but sometimes beauty is in the eye of the beholder. What is possible for you? How will your garden tell your story?

An old wire chair seat brimming with hanging flowers is part of my friend Jane's landscape appeal. She has also been known to hang an antique candelabra in a tree for a cozy summer supper.

Our friend Richard built an alpine creek bed through and around a mound of soil planted with young aspens, then sent water tumbling down the river rocks with an underground pump. The scenic area, a mosaic of sun-dappled foliage, attracts birds and, unfortunately, also many flower-hungry deer. Finding innovative ways to exclude the munching invaders from his landscape becomes simply another part of participating in the landscape of life.

"We are never nowhere," explains Kevin Sharpe, a professor at Union Institute. "From our first environment in our mother's wombs to the last breath we take, we continually interact with the world around us."[6]

The summer I had a large strawberry patch was one of the happiest times of my life. My toddler "worked" beside me, both of us on hands and knees. I was glad when one-year-old Tirza learned that those red squishy shapes tasted good. She quit picking the plants by their roots and plucking off the green fruit. I let her eat her fill until she fell asleep in the grass. Her exhausted sleeping form—backlit by the sun, which shone through a mop of curls—was an icon of that holy place and time. Within a twinkling, it seemed, she was eight and had been joined by two sisters. Still, Tirza led the entrepreneurial effort to pick lemons and limes from our backyard trees and sell them on the street ("Five cents, please"), and a pitcher of homemade lemon-limeade was her idea. Little did it matter to me that the sugar and the paper cups cost far more than would be earned. The pleasure on three cherub faces was my contribution to the world that day. This was the true landscape of my life, sweeter than the scent of the roses along the neighbor's front porch.

Some things we do not produce by conscious effort or design. We simply take our chances, and in brief moments of time, they become the most beautiful art of our lives. It is the human touch, the green thumb, the weathered prayers that fertilize seed.

These gardens start with the landscape you have been given and by letting the story tell itself.

soul PROJECT

Dream a Garden

Is it no small thing," the poet Matthew Arnold asked, "to have enjoyed the sun, to have lived light in the spring?"[7]

Certainly gardens are a green infrastructure of ecological and spiritual prosperity that inspire healthier, more livable communities. Your garden is also a private sanctuary where you can indulge your own sense of connection to the earth. Here you can find tranquility and plant elements of surprise—and did you know you can do all that without spending a fortune or moving a mountain?

Begin by documenting your wildest dreams. Have you yearned to create a butterfly haven? Do you long to grow an exotic kind of rose or to build a lily pond where you can sit every evening at twilight?

Prioritize these dreams and divide into the number of years you expect to live at your current residence. Just have fun with this; nothing about it is set in stone.

Create a calendar for the coming year on which you place photos and visual inspirations—seed packets or photographs—for your dream garden. Write in one or two very simple steps (and the cost) each month that may be possible for you to accomplish.

Enjoy the anticipation, but don't think about how you're going to do it all. Let yourself feel the sensation of accomplishment ahead of time by imagining completed projects. Do what you can, but don't stay attached to a particular outcome or the completion of everything on your calendar. Substitute anything unlikely to be accomplished with smaller similar projects that bring you pleasure.

Work by chiseling down big projects into small steps. Set up an outside area with the tools you will need. Give yourself a time limit each day so you don't become discouraged by obstacles or overwhelmed by the enormity of a particular job.

Remember that the journey is the destination. Work mindfully, knowing that each week's task is changing you as well as your landscape and garden.

When winter rolls around, bring in the outdoors. Decorate with bouquets or leafy branches in watering cans, garden benches along a kitchen wall, or tropical fish in a pretty bowl. Create a garden meditation corner with flowering plants. Add a willow chair with a chintz cushion and a small trickling water feature. Nestle garden-inspired quotes in the corners. Come rain or snow, enjoy your lush little inside Eden.

TWENTY-SEVEN

Storm Shelters
OF THE SPIRIT

It is in the shelter of each other that the people live.

Irish Proverb

My first grade friend Mattie Mae was a happy kid who wore her hair in short braids all over her head, fastened with colorful plastic barrettes. She lived on the other side of the tracks in my small hometown. I discovered this the day I went to her house to play after school. Mattie Mae's prairie-type sod house was buried in the ground like a hobbit's habitat, all covered with grass. Its threshold, however, stood upright in a mound of rounded earth, looking nonsensical and inventive. The door opened to a stairway leading down into a dark room with a bare lightbulb hanging from the ceiling. Apart from this, the brightest thing in the underground room was the smile on the face of Mattie Mae's mother, waiting with cookies and milk.

Before visiting Mattie Mae, I'd seen underground storm shelters on my cousins' farms. These were primitive dugouts covered with a wooden door that lay flush with the ground. In the earlier part of the last century, you had to lift the heavy door of a shelter straight up to slip in under it, and you had to be careful not to squish your fingers when it soundly slammed down. I ventured into a shelter in a game of hide-and-seek. Peeking out through cracks in the wooden door, I shivered from the damp chill of the cave below and the excitement of concealment.

Hiding from a real tornado was never fun and games; in the heartland, storm shelters are not a luxury item. Eight hundred tornadoes a year are reported in the United States, most south of Kansas in Oklahoma and Texas. Twisters cause an average of eighty deaths a year and 1,500 injuries.[1] Releasing raw destructive power, the area receiving the brunt of their devastating energy is called ground zero. Here cattle and trees may be flung like matchsticks. Houses and even entire neighborhoods disappear.

When my family moved to the West Coast, another kind of shelter took the population by storm. The Cold War made Americans feel vulnerable to attack on our own soil, and the Cuban Missile Crisis fueled our national paranoia toward Communism and the threat it represented. We were told that the Soviet Union had nuclear bombs poised toward American cities. Living in a prime target city where U.S. Navy and Marine Corps were based made San Diegans feel especially vulnerable. By 1961 my innocent daily walk to the elementary school became ominous. Pipes sticking out of the ground began to appear in front yards. By each a sign offered notice of a fallout shelter that would provide protection from chemicals and nuclear radiation. At school bomb drills replaced the more mundane earthquake drills. But the defense strategy was no different. We were to immediately take position under our desks—as if that would protect us from bombs or contamination. As an eleven-year-old, I discovered the world was becoming a menacing place.

In troubled times shelters are meant to mitigate the traumatic effects of a disaster. The psalmist's image of shelter as that of God's "wings" implies being able to rise above danger as we are carried up and over the threatening storm. While we may lose control, he never does.[2] Shelters give us a second chance at life. Large, community tornado shelters are rare. The idea of public fallout shelters never took off. But today we have a different kind of public shelter. In the late 1990s, the population of homeless people reached a peak across the United States. But "you don't see homeless people as much as you did in the '80s," reports *Time* magazine, because "the one great policy initiative of the past twenty years has been to move them from grates into the newest form of the poorhouse, the shelter."[3]

The fastest-growing segment of homeless people is mothers with children. This population is undeniably vulnerable in terms of their immediate need. Analysts say that in 2003 the prime cause of homelessness was not alcohol and drugs as many perceived but the lack of affordable housing. This, combined with shamefully low wages for the unskilled, created a dark odyssey for the underside of working America. Stories of real-life single moms were documented by Bill Moyers, spotlighting Oregon's woes. Although heralded for its natural beauty and quality of life, my state is ranked first in "incidents of outright hunger," and it ranks sixth for "food insecurity," meaning people don't know from meal to meal whether they can acquire food for themselves and their families.[4]

Weigh that with journalist Barbara Ehrenreich's discovery in 2003 that "the average woman coming off welfare since 1996 earns $7 an hour—$280/week before taxes," and that "you can't support children on that."[5]

Ehrenreich knows because she tried it. She worked as a waitress, motel maid, and Wal-Mart employee in order to document the problem and found herself able to afford nothing more than a shabby motel room when working for minimum wage. But she considered herself fortunate, because in those motels she met entire families living without a kitchen. With no "real" jobs to go back to, they were also without hope.

As the rift between the affluent and the lower middle class becomes wider, housing prices are driven up. Rent hikes mean many families pay 60 to 75 percent of their income to keep a roof over their heads. Low- and middle-income wage earners are in many places being squeezed out of family-friendly communities. In some towns committees for affordable housing are active. They mandate development of low-income homes for service employees (for example, firemen, grocery clerks, and teachers). But those houses are too often snatched up by retirees or by the wealthy as rentals or vacation residences.[6]

Recently I took a number and a seat in the local Social Security office. The clock ticked impassionedly. The gray walls reflected the stormy sky outside. My plastic chair had a crack in it, so I moved to another behind a jittery teenage couple and their baby boy. The drab office—with its "official" sitting behind a glass window in the middle of one wall—seemed an inappropriate environment in which to take care of personal, and sometimes very private, business. I was there to change my name, a simple straightforward request that carried no baggage or shame. Still, I felt intimidated just by the atmosphere. An occasional rustle of a magazine was the only thing that drowned the strained silence in the room.

A middle-aged woman was sitting in the front row with three daughters. I began to observe this little family, thinking back about twelve years when my own kids were the same ages. Because I've been there, it wasn't hard to recognize telltale signs of on-the-edge survival. The mother looked tired and worried. When she got up to go to the window, her older daughter stuck by her side, listening to everything that was said, a nervous look in her blue eyes. I felt empathy for that girl for having to take on a role she should not have so early in life. She was obviously nervous about the outcome of the meeting. The younger girls, dressed in ill-fitting clothes and shoes, were scuffling around, teasing each other, charming in their own way. The mother looked helpless as she spoke in an earnest tone with the official. The girl by her side turned to scold her sisters. Before long the family trooped out through the heavy door, subdued, the mother looking sadder than ever.

There was a day when I would have wondered how people got themselves into such destitute situations. My former self-righteousness shames me now. Being down and out is not just about wrong choices and lack of faith. I no longer want to be in denial that it can happen to anybody. It happened to me.

At the Social Security office that day, I felt impressed to follow the woman and her children outside to give her some hope. I wanted to know her and hear about her family, but I wasn't sure how to start. I didn't know what to say. I had no cash in my purse, and I didn't want to patronize her.

So I stayed in my chair.

Afterward I realized the only thing I protected was my own dignity. Since then I've been haunted by this family.

Jim Wallis, editor of *Sojourners* magazine, says the theme of wealth and poverty is the second most prominent theme in the Bible (after idolatry). He claims that in our country there is a climate of denial about homelessness. "We must change the culture," he says, because the issues are spiritual, not political.[7]

There are different kinds of homelessness, of course. A home is more than just somewhere to sleep, and making a home takes

227

more than money. Some people have several houses but are never at home. Some, even the educated, are homeless by choice and spurn shelters, preferring instead to sleep on a park bench or under a bridge. Documenting the stories, poets on Skid Row in Los Angeles give voice to all the homeless, telling us they are the face of America. *Street Roots* (see streetroots.org) is dedicated to the idea that the poor provide vital feedback to us all. The paper is devoted to the writings of disenfranchised people on the premise that everyone, despite circumstances, has wisdom and beauty to share.

There is a stigma about not being a "regular" family. But homelessness of any kind must be redefined with the dignity and credibility it deserves. On the premise that we must be the change we want to see in the world, I'm starting with me. This year I'm leaving the house where I raised my children. After a decade of difficult struggle to hang on to this place to give my children roots, I now find a certain delight in the fact that home is not just a physical structure.

Voluntary homelessness for me means packing a small suitcase with jeans, sweaters, boots, and three or four soul-nurturing books. I'm not going to live in the park or in my car. But I am going to experiment with my life, live close to my granddaughter, and see what happens. Vacating the space that has held my hopes for so long, I'm going to transform those hopes into a more solid reality than a physical home could ever be.

A bumper sticker tells me, IF YOU LIVED IN YOUR HEART, YOU'D BE HOME NOW. I believe that. With the wings of the Almighty as shelter, I am taking flight, rising above what I thought I wanted, to a brand-new vision of home.

I once saw on television a ten-year-old girl in a homeless shelter who was wiser than many grown-ups when she remarked, "Oh, we have a home; we just need a house to put it in."

soul PROJECT

Shelter for the Soul

A re you brave enough to take a virtual journey through homelessness?

Here's your chance. An Internet game called Hobson's Choice offers interaction with the big issues by forcing you to make the same kind of choices as a homeless person. Log on to Realchangenews.org to play Hobson's Choice, and you'll quickly find yourself facing hard decisions.

The point, however, is to keep trying, say the game's originators. You'll discover that things that don't work for you the first time you try them may work out on the tenth try or the fourteenth try. Hobson's Choice gives anyone an opportunity to step into a homeless person's shoes and learn about the reality of life on the streets, and its multiple discouragements.

Hobson's Choice hopes to increase the voice of the marginalized and break down stereotypes. And it could do something on a higher plane if you follow the observations of Jim Wallis, author of *Who Speaks for God?* "The real ecumenism of the past 25 years," Wallis says, "has taken place in soup kitchens and homeless shelters more than at tables of theologians trying to find unity on the meaning of the Eucharist."[8]

TWENTY-EIGHT

Fiddling on
THE ROOF

Ripping off the roof of my faith-home should not be an experimental exercise, but a permanent spiritual condition. I now desire to keep the roof open to the heavens.... Spiritual life has to be open to the changes from above, beneath and from the outside.

Arthur Paul Patterson

Weather patterns shift. Beams are tested. Shingles cling tenaciously to their places. Time moves forward. Things change. We are "as shaky as a fiddler on the roof," says Broadway character Tevye about our precarious lives. The script implies that it is only with great balance that we play out our existence. This seems as true today as it did under czarist rule in Anatevica, Russia, in 1905. We still wrestle with issues of family and faith. Our reality is simply set in a different cultural context.

The presence of the fiddler is a symbol of the part tradition plays in the story. As the lowliest of musicians in Russian Jewish soul music, the fiddler was a near social outcast. As Tevye makes the best of his harsh existence, the fiddler on the roof often puts into words what he cannot say. At times it seems Tevye would like to escape to the rooftop himself.

We all know how it feels, as the lyrics to that James Taylor hit go, "when this old world starts a'getting me down."

The refrain: "Up on the roof!"

Clinging to existence in the floods of trouble, a rooftop is sometimes the only place we have to go. In much the same way, rare Atlantic shorebirds have resorted to nesting on rooftops along the East Coast, crowded away from beaches by sunbathers and Frisbee players. Nearly hunted to extinction at the turn of the twentieth century for their feathers, an adornment for women's hats, the birds are no longer welcome on the sand. Gravel roofs have become a critical safety net for them, say scientists.

Rooftops have always made for great getaways. Growing up in his family's Victorian-era estate in the South, my friend Wills used to escape to the attic and then crawl from a small window onto the roof of the house. He would carefully close the window behind him in case anyone came looking. The rooftop was a place for pondering and for experiencing the seductive thrill of hiding out. Rooftops lure as a place to connect with something bigger than ourselves, a skill we develop as children and will need the rest of our lives.

For me that means practice at not being scared to death. I never climbed on a roof as a child but nowadays do it twice a year to sweep away the cushy layer of pine needles that continually fall. My roof is not a steep slope. Still, walking down toward the edge of the roofline where most of the needles settle is one of the more discomfiting things I do. The rooftop exercise reminds me that fear is either a gift or an illusion. You need to know the difference, but if you trust your skill of discernment and the solid place under your feet, you can pretty much do whatever you set your mind to do.

I tie up my athletic shoes and, dragging my rake and broom, climb the ladder to the lowest eave of my house. Crunching around on the shake shingles, I look down through the skylights into my dining room and think of the various scenarios that have been played out there over the years. I remember wondering if the girls and I would make it safe and sound. Every night I prayed that angels would protect our home, and I prayed for my girls, for my livelihood, and for courage. Now, looking back, having "been there, done that," I am thankful. The roof still stands. All is well.

But all is not finished. The rooftop is a place to see the horizon. I look for the snow-covered mountaintops beyond tall pines and appreciate the wild perimeters of my property. Horizons are all around us, of course, and they change whenever we view them from a different vantage point.

On my rooftop this spring, cleaning off another accumulation of pine needles, I realized that with one task behind me (raising kids), I am facing another. Equally daunting is that of seeking a new adventure and place to invest my energy. Once again I face the same old fears. Once again I plant my two feet securely under me and stand firm. I have learned to trust the process. I have learned to trust in God. I have learned to trust my own agility to move around in scary places.

I was mesmerized by the beautiful chase scenes with leaping, running, and dancing across rooftops in the martial arts fantasy *Crouching Tiger, Hidden Dragon*. What would it be like if we were empowered to fight our own threatening enemies in such graceful slow motion? Sometimes when processing fear, obstacles, or challenges, I've found it helpful to imagine what things may look like from a different perspective. Sometimes I turn the paradigms upside down. For example, how might things be different if rooftops were the ground?

In Toronto, some residents have imagined just that and have made a profit. They've taken to rooftop gardening. To make agriculture feasible in the city, rooftops were envisioned as available growing space for vegetables. Container gardening on top of human-made structures is well established in Europe. In Canada the experiment is going well, and buyers are already waiting for the next harvest. The Fairmont Waterfront Hotel in Vancouver, jumping in with both feet, now grows some of the veggies and flowers it needs on its accessible roof. The savings is an estimated $30,000 per year in food costs.[1]

Architects in San Francisco came up with another kind of environmentally friendly roof. At Golden Gate Park, four acres of greenery were added atop a new home for the California Academy of Sciences. An Italian architect designed a grass-top roof with undulating contours of various heights to imitate the fabled topography of the city on the bay. What a switch from rooftop "*park*ing" in premium downtown areas across our country!

Rooftops have been the subject of songs, movies, and books, often representing our highest aspirations, usually of a spiritual kind. Mary Poppins's friend, the chimney sweep, delighted in his domain between pavement and stars on the rooftops of London. On the opposite side of the spectrum, the novel *Grass Roof, Tin Roof* by Dao Strom is about cultural clash and the spiritual aftermath of war. The image of roof is metaphor for sacred places and the communication of lofty ideas. Tibet, known as the "roof of the world," is a place of pilgrimage and the setting for history, adventure, and devotion.

233

What we know as Gothic architecture, famed for its elaborate and ornamental steeply pitched roofs (and whimsical gargoyles), was a biblical script for its day (AD 1150–1300). Built before the printing press, its cathedrals were a substitute for books. Gothic cathedrals were written in symmetry and a sacred code. Revolutionary for its time, this medieval building concept focused on supportive framework instead of walls. Piers, arches, and buttresses supported heavy roofs made of limestone, lead, tile, or slate. What we call "balanced thrust" produced perfect equilibrium to keep the roof aloft. It also created the faith-lifting inspiration of strong vertical lines. As one of humanity's most successful architectural experiments, the vaulted roofs spanned great open spaces. On holy festival days, these were filled by an entire city standing shoulder to shoulder. The sublimity of the great vertical lines affected the soul even before the art of windows and façades was noticed.[2]

In brutal contrast, I once lived in a house in Bethlehem where the absolutely flat roof also served as a place of worship. I had my private quiet time there daily. But its view was of numerous levels of hillsides filled with other concrete houses. And I could see rooftop upon rooftop where laundry was hung and where women carried out their work and built community in the process.

Not far away, but 1,400 years earlier, St. Abba Dorotheus founded a monastery in Gaza. In his primer for spiritual training, he wrote: "The ordinary house has a roof. The roof of the soul's house is love, which is the perfection of the virtues, just as the roof of a house is the completion of the house."[3]

When we gather under a roof, help raise a roof, work hard to put a roof over our children's heads, we are saying this is the place where we belong, and this is what love is.

The structure above us represents what we want, what we know for sure, and what we hope will last; the roof is the crowning glory of our home. To come in under its shelter each evening is both our reward and the summit of experience on earth. It brings to a successful conclusion the calling of our lives out and about in the world. Under the roof we find privacy, community, and shelter from storm; most important, we come back full circle to ourselves and those we love.

Shout it from the rooftops: There is no place like home.

My Living SPACES

Once upon a time you may have dreamed of the home where you live now. Perhaps you're dreaming of a different home in a different place. In either case, dreams—and homes—change and evolve, but the dreams always need to be fed and watered. Use these pages to note things you hope your home will be. Write your heart out as you discover more about where you live, what's possible there, and what you really want. *Ah, there's no place like home.*

_____

_____

_____

_____

_____

_____

_____

_____

_____

_____

_____

_____

_____

_____

_____

My Living SPACES

My Living SPACES

My Living SPACES

My Living SPACES

My Living SPACES

Notes

Welcome: An Invitation

1. John 14:23, paraphrased.

Chapter 2: Romancing the Hearth

1. Proverbs 31:10–31, paraphrased and condensed.

Chapter 3: No Copycat Corridor

1. Bill Sporito, "Inside the New American Home," *Time*, October 14, 2002, 67, 70, 73.

Chapter 6: Walls Have Ears

1. Isaiah 54:2.
2. Laura Cerwinske, *In a Spiritual Style* (New York: Thames and Hudson, 1998), 13.
3. Sue Monk Kidd, *The Secret Life of Bees* (New York: Penguin, 2002), 2.
4. Sheila Bridges, "Places of the Heart," *Victoria*, October 2002, 42.
5. John 21:25.

Chapter 7: Not Your Granny's Nooks and Crannies

1. Marlee Alex, "Risky Business," *Aspire*, April/May 1999, 23.

2. A. A. Milne, "Halfway Down," *The World of Christopher Robin* (New York: Dutton, 1958).

Chapter 8: Hot Pot Haven

1. Genesis 18:1.

2. John 21:17.

3. Matthew 10:42.

Chapter 9: Table d'hôte

1. Kelee Katillac, *House of Belief* (Layton, UT: Gibbs-Smith, 2000), 17.

Chapter 10: Great Room, Good Living

1. Paul Tournier, *A Place for You* (New York: Harper and Row, 1968), 15.

Chapter 13: Soulful, Sensual Bathing

1. Mikkel Aaland, *Sweat* (Santa Barbara: Capra, 1978) quoted in "The 'Turkish Bath' Visits Europe and North America," 1997, www.cyberbohemia.com/Pages/TBINUSA.htm.

Chapter 14: Home Office, Postmodern Hearth

1. "IFMA Survey Ranks Top 10 Office Complaints," press release, June 2003, www.automatedbuildings.com/release/iuno3/ifma.htm.

2. Mary Englebriet, greeting card (Kansas City: Andrews and McMeel).

Chapter 15: Remodeling the Dream

1. Deuteronomy 33:24–25.

2. Psalm 119:105.

3. Romans 10:15; cf. Isaiah 52:7.

4. Revelation 10:1.

5. Genesis 28:16.

6. David Fontana, *The Secret Language of Dreams* (San Francisco: Chronicle Books, 1994), 18.

7. John 14:2.

8. Revelation 21:19–21.

9. Fontana, *The Secret Language of Dreams*, 5.

10. Frank Garfield and Rhondda Stewart-Garfield, *Dreams* (New York: Barnes and Noble, 1998), 95–97.

Chapter 16: Dollhouses: Dreams in Miniature

1. Dominique Browning, *Around the House and in the Garden* (New York: Scribner, 2002), 198.

2. William L. Hamilton, "House and Home/Style Desk," *New York Times*, August 15, 2002, 2.

Chapter 17: Finding Your Tribe: The Nomad in You

1. David Levinson and David Sherwood, *The Tribal Living Book* (Boulder, CO: Johnson Books, 1993).

2. Ice Hotel homepage, www.icehotel-canada.com.

Chapter 18: A Tree House Takes a Bough

1. Suki Casanave, "Tree Houses Take a Bough," *Smithsonian*, August 1997, www.Smithsonianmag.si.edu/smithsonian/issues97/aug97/treehouses.html.

2. Jonathan Fairoaks, homepage, Livingtreeonline.com.

3. Proverbs 3:18.

4. Shel Silverstein, "Tree House," *Where the Sidewalk Ends* (New York: Harper & Row, 1974), 79.

Chapter 19: A Cave Dweller's Penthouse Paradox

1. Djuna Bewley and Dave Bunnell, "Virtual Cave," December 2003, www.goodearthgraphics.com/virtcave.

2. Romans 7:19–24.

3. Rolland Hein, *The Harmony Within* (Chicago: Cornerstone Press, 1999), 112.

4. J. M. Barrie, *Peter Pan*, www.bibliomania.com/0/0/323/2396/27548/1.html.

5. Mick Cope, "Leading through Conversations—Shadows," www.WizOz.co.uk.

6. Joan Anderson, *A Year by the Sea* (New York: Broadway, 2000), 115.

7. Debbie Ford, *The Dark Side of the Light Chasers* (New York: Riverhead, 1998), 2.

8. Anna G. Edmonds, *Turkey's Religious Sites* (Istanbul: A. S. Damko, 1997), 194–95.

9. Ibid., 198.

10. "The Catacombs of Saint Callixtus," March 7, 2003, www.Catacombe.roma.it/en/cal.html.

Chapter 20: Crenellated Castles in the Air

1. Walfram von Eschenbach, *Parzival*, trans. A. T. Hatto (New York: Penguin, 1980).

2. Clarissa Pinkola Estes, *Women Who Run with the Wolves* (New York: Ballantine Books, 1995), 39–73.

Chapter 21: The Art of Living Interiors

1. Gail Mayhugh, "Five Secrets to Model Home Design," www.GMJInteriors.com (site now discontinued).

2. Diane Wintroub Calmenson, "The Language of Color," Isdesignet.com magazine, October 2000.

3. "Bestselling Colors for 2002," www.colormarketing.org.

4. Quoted in Catherine Murrell, "Contemporary African Art Helps People Express Life," *The Courier Journal*, October 20, 2001.

5. Jane Alexander, *Spirit of the Home* (New York: Watson Guptill Publications, 1995).

6. Ken Burns, "The Master Builders," *Vanity Fair*, November 1988, 302–18.

7. Mary Groves, interview by Marlee LeDai, 2003, Bend, OR.

Chapter 22: Keep a Beacon Burning

1. "Lighthouses," June 11, 2001, www.grandespirito.it/inglese .farieng.html.

2. Larry Walker, "We'll Keep the Light On for You," October 2002, www.Neusesailing.org.

3. Matthew 25:1–13.

4. Angus Macleod, "It Lasts Forever," *The Silent Ones* (Torquil Productions, 1999). Used by permission.

5. Matthew 5:14–16.

Chapter 23: Beautiful Borders and Boundaries

1. Dorothy Folz-Gray, "Life in the Garden," HGTV, *Ideas* magazine, 2004, www.HGTV.com.

2. Clare Cooper Marcus, *House as a Mirror of Self* (Berkeley: Conari Press, 1997), 63.

3. Isaiah 54:2 NIV.

Chapter 24: Gear Up for Garages

1. Kira Obolensky, *Garage, Reinventing the Place We Park* (Newton, CT: The Taunton Press, 2001), 7.

Chapter 25: Porch Swingers and Other Plucky People

1. Wynonna Judd, "Grandpa (Tell Me 'Bout the Good Old Days)," *The Judds Collection*, Wynonna, Inc., 1992. Words and music by Jamie O'Hara.

2. Daniel Redwood, "Creating an Imaginative Life," www.Bewell naturally.net.

Chapter 26: Landscape Love Songs

1. Kari West, "Garden Glories," www.Gardenglories.com.

2. Judy Valente, "Celtic Spirituality," *Religion and Ethics Weekly*, week 428, www.PBS.org.

3. Ibid.

4. Henry David Thoreau, essay title unknown.

5. Dominique Browning, *Around the House and in the Garden* (New York: Scribner, 2002), 113.

6. Kevin Sharpe, "Spirit of Place," Certificate in Science and Spirituality Online Courses, Union Institute and University, Cincinnati, OH, 2003.

7. Matthew Arnold, from the "Hymn of the Empedocles," *The Oxford Book of English Verse 1250–1900*, edited by Arthur Quiller-Couch, 1919.

Chapter 27: Storm Shelters of the Spirit

1. National Weather Service, www.adem.state.ar.us.com.

2. Psalm 61:4.

3. Joel Stein, "The Real Face of Homelessness," *Time*, January 20, 2003.

4. Bill Moyers, "Nickle and Dimed in America," *Now*, March 29, 2002, www.PBS.org/now/transcriptlll-full.html.

5. Ibid.

6. Julia Silverman, "Retirees Push School Kids Out," *Associated Press*, April 2003.

7. Jim Wallis, "Time to Come to Washington," May/June 2002, *Sojourners*, www.sojo.net.

8. Jim Wallis, "All Together Now," May/June 1997, *Sojourners*, www.sojo.net.

Chapter 28: Fiddling on the Roof

1. "Green Roofs for Healthy Cities," *Better Times: The Webzine*, www.Justpeace.org/better02-20-2000.htm.

2. Emile Male, *The Gothic Image* (New York: Harper Torchbooks, 1958), 398–99.

3. Christian Classics, "St. Abba Dorotheus of Gaza," 2001, www .touchstonemag.com.

Acknowledgments

My heartfelt thanks go to my editor and darling friend, Jeanette Thomason, who imagined this book into being with me. Her artful originality is its foundation.

To my daughters, the three graces, goes the credit of inspiration. Tirza, Leyah, and Lissa, I'm honored to have shared life and love under the same roof with you for so many years.

To each and every individual and family whose threshold I've crossed, you'll find your fingerprints on these pages; thank you!

Marlee LeDai . . .

is an author of more than twenty-five books. As an editor and writer, she has contributed to many more, including *Keeper of the Springs*, with Ingrid Trobisch; Tyndale's *The Family Bible*; Focus on the Family's *Caring for Aging Loved Ones*; and books by Barbara Johnson.

With her third infant on her knee, Marlee translated the stories of Hans Christian Andersen from old-world Danish into English—and contributed to other best-selling editions (more than 7 million books sold). Her children's book *Grandpa and Me: We Learn About Death* received the C. S. Lewis Gold Medallion Award.

Marlee was editor and columnist of *Virtue* magazine and a contributing editor to *Aspire* magazine. Writing for a variety of other magazines and online sites, she's published more than 150 articles, cover stories, and interviews. She teaches on the spiritual voices of women at Writers.com, and she helped launch two websites: the American Bible Society's ForMinistry.com, and Damarisproject.org, sponsored by the Damaris Project, which seeks to nurture faith in America's educated professional women.

Marlee is on the executive board of Freedom in the Son, Inc., a ministry to incarcerated women serving Oregon's female inmates. She is a spiritual director, trained by the Art of Sacred Living Center in Bend, Oregon. Speaking about making a house a home, travel, and life pilgrimage, she leads workshops for women in transition and serves as a mentor on moving forward.

With an eye on stories that offer healing and inspiration, Marlee has lived and worked in a variety of places abroad, including Francis and Edith Schaeffer's L'Abri community in the Swiss Alps. As a journalist, she's traveled widely in Israel (between the Munich massacre and the Yom Kippur War); behind the Iron Curtain (during the Cold War); to Haiti (during the U.S. embargo); through Turkey's religious sites; and along Normandy's D-Day trail, interviewing both locals and American veterans for the anniversary celebration.

Marlee's love of family, adventure, and women's culture characterize her life. Now a grandmother, she enjoys hiking, fly fishing, and snowboarding in Oregon and Northern California, where she lives.

Leyah Jensen . . .

is a children's book designer for Scholastic Publishing. In her free time she writes and illustrates. As Marlee LeDai's middle daughter, she's helped the author rearrange many a room, set and clear many a table, and gaze up at a summer night's stars from sleeping bags in the backyard. Yes, she admits, some of the fingerprints in the hallway are hers.

Having moved away from the sleepy mountain town of Sisters, Oregon, Leyah now lives in New York City. Stars have been replaced with city lights, and homes must be made in apartment buildings among strangers. But while illustrating this book, she remembered the meaning of home as taught by her mother and as she painted in makeshift gardens built on empty lots. She was inspired by the tender placement of discarded materials among flower beds: an upright bedspring to support a curling vine, or a broken chandelier becoming prisms in a tree. She believes that wherever we are, home is where we grow dreams from our life's story.

If you liked LIVING SPACES,
you'll love Marlee's next book:

Go, Girl

FINDING ADVENTURE WHEREVER THE ROAD LEADS

In stores April 2005